"I have known Todd and Laura Shoemaker for about ten years. I first met Todd on a video shoot for our church. We immediately bonded. I attribute that mostly to our shared passion for Christ. We also both went to the same college, albeit at different times.

I asked some people about Todd and they told me he was "salt of the earth" and that Laura was a saint. Years later, I can confirm this is true. I'm a better Christian today because I am friends with the Shoemakers.

From Todd, I've learned to always trust God. For as long as I've known Todd, he's had physical limitations. He was supposed to die multiple times. His attitude is, I guess God isn't done with me yet. He continues to fight human trafficking with a fervor few people have. Whenever Todd goes to the hospital, he just assumes he's supposed to share Christ with someone.

From Laura, I've learned self-sacrifice. I'm sure she has moments when she's not smiling, but I've never seen one. She is still madly in love with Todd, and he is madly in love with her. Todd and Laura are perfectly matched. I'm honored to call them friends."

Steve Scalici,
Pastor, Family Church Jupiter

"Todd and Laura are the heroes every inner-city youth would be blessed to have. They've been in my corner when I needed them most and are still there supporting me. I wouldn't be the man I am today apart from their faithful love, wisdom, and support. Having access to such Overcomers instilled the value of resilience in me, which characterizes my life today. I am a Hope Dealer today because Todd and Laura gave me hope!"

Ricky Aiken,
Founder and Executive Director, Inner City Innovators

"Todd Shoemaker's relentless and selfless crusade to serve Jesus is both inspirational and personally impactful. This Palm Beach Atlantic University alumnus is a courageous warrior, who is consistently focused on others. His faith, as described in his book, is contagious. Catch it!"

Dr. Bill Fleming,
President, Palm Beach Atlantic University

"Todd has suffered more in his adult life than almost anybody I know. Yet he maintains a posture of positivity, encouragement, and love. He doesn't draw attention to himself and he doesn't complain. As one of his pastors, it is a bittersweet honor for me to observe his character and commitment to Christ."

Jimmy Scroggins,
Lead Pastor, Family Church

"*Tenacious. Conqueror. Superhero. Just a few words to describe Todd's selfless drive for life! If you ever felt like giving up, read this book. The journey towards hope and healing is life changing.*"

Tina Levene,
Author and Motivational Speaker

"*The shortest distance between two people is a good story. This one is incredible, a blueprint to a better life. You will embrace 'The Blessed Overcomer' like a friend you won't want to leave.*"

Bob Dotson,
New York Times Best Selling Author of "American Story, a Lifetime Search for Ordinary People Doing Extraordinary Things."

"*Scrappy* was Todd's nickname in college. It is somewhat symbolic of the tenacity and fighting spirit that is so prevalent in his current health battle. Much is learned about a person's character during tough times and his is more than evident. *Scrappy* is truly *OC!*"

Ben Starling, III
Southern Philanthropy, Inc.

"*I have known Todd & Laura for a number of years, I consider them to be great friends. With that said, I have had a front row seat to their journey. Watching the way that Todd & Laura navigate Todd's health struggle has really been inspirational. Although my friend Todd is a medical mystery, it is no mystery who he lives for and represents daily. It is for the love of his wife and for the fame and glory of God.*"

Proverb Newsome,
Musician, Author, Podcaster

"I have always admired Todd's courage through the physical battles he has faced. Even in the midst of severe challenge, he always prioritizes the growth of his faith. He is a positive, affirming, and steadfast man of God. And no matter how weak he may be, his commitment to press on and fully engage in worship and service to our Lord is a source of encouragement to myself and others.

Todd is an overcomer and he has made a bold statement for the Kingdom with his life. He and Laura are dear to my and Donna's hearts. We all can learn from and be inspired by their story."

Tom Mullins,
Founding Pastor, Christ Fellowship Church

The Blessed Overcomer

By Todd and Laura Shoemaker

RoseDale
COMMUNICATIONS

Graphics and cover by Amber Patrick, at GNE Design & Photography

Literary consulting services and editing provided by Clara Rose of RoseDale Communications. Published by RoseDale Publishing, an imprint of RoseDale Communications, Inc.

ISBN: 978-0-9975120-4-5

Dedication

This book is dedicated to our moms, Carmen West and Brenda Shoemaker, the dynamic duo. They lovingly care for us, through thick and thin, with lots of laughter along the way.

Also, to Team Blessed Overcomer, too many people to name. Thank you for walking with us through this crazy, beautiful journey.

SHOEMAKER

Contents

Acknowledgments

We want to acknowledge RoseDale Communication for their commitment to this project. They have brought us joy in completing this project.

Amber Patrick at GNE Design & Photography for her tireless work on our incredible graphics designs. Her love and talent have amazed us, and we are grateful for her contributions.

Gene Bergman at 1331 Kreative for his amazing video productions promoting this project. His friendship, walking along side of us, has made a lasting impression. His video talent has been so creative and appreciated.

Carmen Faith Ward, our sister and social media guru. Her dedication to this project and endless social media support has been amazing. She is one of our biggest cheerleaders.

Jean Brown, our faithful traveling companion. On the many road trips to cross-country appointments, Jean taught us about "Elevenses" (the most delicious break of the morning, enjoying a snack and tea). She always provides a wonderful home-away-from-home when Laura needs a place to stay while I'm in the hospital. She takes such great care of us, and we couldn't do it without her.

Our West and Shoemaker families have loved and supported us tremendously. Their support has carried us through tough times.

Our medical teams over the past 17 years. We have received incredible care and we are grateful for their commitment.

Our second family at Good Samaritan Medical Center on 4 South, has always gone above and beyond in quality service and personal care.

Our Family Church and Christ Fellowship families have given us an outpouring measure of love, prayers, and support. We have been in need, over the years, during difficult times. They have been so supportive, providing just what we need.

Rework new
with detail

Introduction

Not everyone who reads our story is interested in the details, such as the dates of a diagnosis, the type of diagnosis, or the actual treatments. That's okay, we wrote this book to encourage others who are going through the storms of life, the details of the journey are not as important as the sharing of hope.

If you are one of those people who DO want the details, I am happy to share those with you. It started with a single misdiagnosis and continues as new challenges and issues have become a part of our lives.

I was originally diagnosed with several forms of crippling arthritis. The rheumatologist had me on several medications and expected me to be in a wheelchair within 5 years. It was not exactly the future I had imagined, and I intended to prove him wrong.

In August of 2003 I was diagnosed with Thymus Cancer. Thymus issues can cause arthritic-like symptoms, which explains the misdiagnosis of arthritis. We opted for surgery as a treatment, and after my recovery I was declared cancer-free. It seemed like we had weathered the big storm and, praise God, we made it through.

After collapsing at home, Thanksgiving of 2004, I was admitted to the hospital. The doctors thought I had all the signs of Myasthenia Gravis, a long-term neuromuscular disease that leads to varying degrees of skeletal muscle weakness. Of course, after that I was off to the specialist again for more testing. When the specialist learned that I was a runner, he said it was NOT possible to have MG and be a runner. So, it was decided that I did not have MG after all.

The diagnosis of Early-Onset Parkinson's came in September of

2007 and shook us up a bit. This is a long-term degenerative disorder of the central nervous system, that mainly affects the motor system. As a runner, this one hit me hard. I loved running and could not imagine a future without it.

March of 2009 the diagnosis of Myasthenia Gravis was confirmed. Runner or not, I indeed had MG. An interesting twist, usually having your thymus removed is a treatment FOR Myasthenia Gravis. Apparently, I fall into a small group of people who get MG AFTER having their thymus removed. Go figure.

One of the most interesting health challenges started in 2015 when I was diagnosed with Gastroparesis. You will learn more in my story about how God prepared me for this one! This medical condition is the paralysis of the stomach, resulting in food remaining in the stomach instead of moving down into the small intestines as it should. It causes an assortment of issues and discomfort.

In October of that year it was decided that I needed a Gastro pacemaker, to assist with the constant nausea associated with the condition. Thankfully, the pacemaker did its job!

When my weight hit an all-time low of 112 pounds, the decision was made to give me a feeding tube. I was still not able to eat, and my body would need to be nourished. March 2017, I received my first feeding tube, and I continue to feed my body in this way. Sometimes when we are at a restaurant, we joke with the waitress that it's *not my turn to eat. We* get the craziest looks from people!

Time passes and we are grateful for every day together. It is 2019 and we still face new challenges as my health issues progress.

We call our life the crazy, beautiful journey because we never know what the new day will bring. Perhaps we should have called this book The Blessed OVERCOMERS since my lovely wife has overcome obstacles herself during this crazy, beautiful journey. This is our story, we pray that this encourages and gives you hope!

SHOEMAKER

Chapter One

A Beautiful Interruption

"Wow, this is going to be a story to tell!"

If you've ever experienced a trip to an amazing destination, you know the feeling of excitement and expectation that grows as you prepare for the journey. In the summer of 2002, as I was getting ready for a mission trip to the Big Apple with about 400 middle and high schoolers, all I could think was, "Wow, this is going to be a story to tell!" Little did I know, this trip was the beginning of my crazy, beautiful journey.

If you're like most people, right about now you are wondering why on earth anyone would want to go on a trip with hundreds of youth. Let me tell you a little about how I arrived here.

In 1991, I found myself an illustrious graduate of Palm Beach Atlantic University. The Gulf War had recently ended, the economy was rough, and jobs were hard to come by. I was a college graduate with little work experience, and let's just say I wasn't prepared for life after college. For the next year, I filled out application after application, and sent resume after resume, only to receive rejection after rejection. *Good thing one of my majors was theater. I was used to rejection.*

Humor aside, I was discouraged and wondering... *why did I even go to college... maybe I should have majored in something else...* and the existential question many young adults are asking... *am I going to live with my parents forever?!?*

Everything changed one afternoon when my dad turned to me and said, "Hey, Todd, my boss knows about a possible job opportunity for you." I called his boss that evening and found out it was a job working with at-risk youth in a residential setting.

It was not quite what I had been looking for, but I considered it and realized I might enjoy the opportunity. *Yeah*, I thought to myself, *I could see myself working with at-risk youth.*

I'd spent countless hours shooting hoops and chatting about school and life with younger kids in the neighborhood throughout my high school and college years. I had also participated in the Workship program at Palm Beach Atlantic University (a community service-based program to assist students in discovering their vocation while developing a life-long habit of servant leadership) and volunteered with youth in the community.

Even though I didn't have professional experience, I went out on a limb and applied for the job. Much to my amazement, I received a phone call to schedule an interview!

As I drove there, I reviewed all that my professors in college had taught me about nailing an interview. The first thing I saw when I walked into the office was a photo of Rod Stewart hanging on the wall, and I immediately knew I had found something of common interest. Turns out we were both huge fans and we spent the first thirty minutes laughing and talking about Rod Stewart. I found out later that this was the only reason I got the job.

Unknown to me, my first boss didn't like my dad's boss and I had used him as a reference. She had arrived with no intention of hiring me, but by the end of the interview, I had landed my first job out of college. This was my start in a career that spanned twenty years working with at-risk youth, and I loved it!! Thank you, Sir Rod Stewart, for intervening on my behalf!

So, on June 29, 2002, with a few hundred middle and high school students, and a few other chaperones, we embarked on a mission to minister to the broken and hurting of New York City. As the jet rose over Palm Beach International Airport, I looked out my window at the sunny, South Florida sky and thought, *Let the adventure begin.*

I knew for certain this was going to be the trip of a lifetime. I was surrounded by hundreds of youth. I had never been to a city this large. Just imagine, I was about to experience the sites, and help the people of New York City! And the food... when I was planning my trip, nearly everyone I spoke to who had visited this great city gave me the name of a restaurant I just had to check out and a reminder, "You have to try the pizza. New York City pizza is the best in the world."

I had every intention of tasting everything I could get my hands on, and warned Laura before I left, "I might come home with an extra fifty pounds."

We arrived in New York later that afternoon. To this day, I can close my eyes and recall the smells and sounds of the city. I had expected to be intimidated, but I was excited! If Facebook Live had been around at the time, I would have gone live and shared my amazing experiences!

We headed to our hotel, unpacked, went over some rules, and then hit the big city to find some *fooood*. I was pretty sure I'd already gained ten pounds just thinking about it!

My group and I walked around wide-eyed for a while before we chose to eat at the ESPN Zone. I know, I know. Really? The ESPN Zone? Of all the restaurants you could choose in New York City, but hey, I was with a bunch of teenage boys. Honestly, I don't even remember what we ate, and none of us really cared. We were in New York City and loving it!!

After we headed back to our hotel that night, and I settled my students in, I went to spend some time with God. I was in the middle of telling him how excited I was when I felt a strong impression that He wanted me to fast. As in, don't eat food!

At first, I thought, *Sure, I can skip breakfast tomorrow morning and spend some extra time with You.*

But God wasn't asking me to fast one meal, He wanted me to fast the entire week. I had never in my life fasted for an entire week!

I had a few more thoughts.

I'm in New York City, and it's the middle of summer.

I'm responsible for hundreds of students, and I need to keep up my energy.

And last, but by no means least... *I need to get through my restaurant list!!*

After what seemed like wrestling with God for hours, I finally gave in and agreed. I knew I would never make it through the week without His help. I prayed, *God, this isn't at all what I expected, but I will obey and fast this week, trusting You for the strength to do it.*

I had a strong sense that God was calling me to fast, because He was preparing me for something. I had no idea what to expect, but I trusted and chose to be obedient.

Sometimes when I talk about fasting, people look at me like I am speaking a foreign language. A fast is the giving up of something valuable or necessary for a period. It is usually done with the belief in mind that the one who is fasting will learn something in return.

Believe it or not, the fast wasn't difficult, and I never felt hungry!

Some days, Laura and I laugh at the irony! I now have a medical condition that prevents me from eating a single bite.

Even without the food, the week was filled with wonderful moments and memories. Less than a year after 9/11, our students ministered love and compassion to the still grieving people of a broken city. We talked, cried, and laughed with many whose lives had been devastated.

The remains of the tragedy of 9/11 were still there, and the city worked day and night to clear the debris and continue to search for loved ones lost. Families stood side by side with pictures in hand; some were still searching, others just wanted to share their stories.

It was a scene that overwhelmed everyone who set foot there. Even the middle schoolers stood reverently without speaking a word. It was as if we were standing on holy ground; it was a place where all the best and the worst of humanity had left its mark.

I felt like a true New Yorker as we stood at Ground Zero.

We were as entertained by the traditions of the New York Yankees fans as they were by our "southern accents" when we witnessed the New York Yankees beat the Cleveland Indians at Yankee Stadium on a warm July night. And oh, what a night it was! The crowd roared when the home team slid into home plate. The noise was deafening when they chanted, "Take the wave back to Shea!"

The pride New Yorkers had in their players was evident as they shouted the names of their favorites, and when the great Bernie Williams responded by turning and tipping his hat to the crowd, the applause shook the stadium.

My students convinced me the hamburgers and hot dogs were the tastiest they had ever eaten. I can't say for certain if it's true, or if the amazing excitement of the night was simply a seasoning that couldn't be matched.

Our trip ended on July 6, 2002, when we flew home to West Palm Beach, Florida. There is no doubt every one of us left a part of ourselves in the Big Apple.

As soon as I was home, I began to prepare for summer camp which was just a few weeks away. I know, crazy, right?!? Yet, I hung out with 500 middle and high school students in the blistering heat of Florida summer, and I enjoyed every minute of it!!

As the summer of 2002 came to an end, I was feeling exhausted and ached from head to toe. But, let's face it, I wasn't twenty any more, and the summer had been crazy, busy, and fun!

I spent the summer watching for my BIG WHY and was still wondering why God had called me to fast, without a clue in sight. Yet, I remained steadfastly certain there was a purpose. I had no idea my story was just beginning – a story of encouragement that would give hope and inspire others to focus on the positive during difficulties and despair.

"Consider it a sheer gift, friends,
when tests and challenges come at you from all sides.
You know that under pressure, your faith-life
is forced into the open and shows its true colors.
So, don't try to get out of anything prematurely.
Let it do its work, so you become mature
and well-developed, not deficient in any way."

James 1:2-4

Laura's Story

While Todd was experiencing the Big Apple, my mom came to town to spend some time with me. Every evening the phone would ring, and her favorite son-in-law would be on the other end. Technically he's her only son-in-law, but eh, details, details.

We looked forward to the daily updates; Todd shared the details and highlights of his trip, and it was a lot of fun living vicariously through his adventures. Every conversation included prayer, and we bonded through the shared experiences.

But Todd wasn't the only one having the time of his life! Mom and I were busy with shopping adventures of our own. While we were out on the town, we found a treasure trove of purchasing pleasure.

The Hallmark store was having a whopping sale - 80% off everything in stock! What woman in her right mind could pass up the opportunity?

Not me, and not my mom! We loaded our baskets with every gift imaginable. By the time Todd arrived home from New York, the entire living room floor was covered with our loot and there was barely a place to step. Mom and I giggled and giggled as we watched Todd attempt to maneuver his luggage through the house.

It was a bit of a fiasco, but the good news is we had about seven to eight hundred dollars' worth of treasure for only a couple hundred dollars, and we had gifts for years! I may even still have a few of those gifts in a closet or two.

Chapter Two

An Unexpected Promise

Love the quote from the author or the poem from ... (handwritten annotation)

"It's a Tumor!"

As my adventurous summer ended, and life returned to "normal," my energy level continued to plummet. With each day, I became more and more fatigued. I just couldn't bounce back.

Laura began to encourage me, "Babe, I really think you should go see a doctor."

Seriously, I didn't even have a primary care doctor. I couldn't recall the last time I'd been sick, but you know how loving wives can be... well let's just say…. relentless. So, to Laura's primary I went.

After a complete physical and a full battery of tests, I was referred to a rheumatologist which meant another round of tests. I was stunned by the results.

"You have several forms of crippling arthritis," the doctor shared with me. "I expect you to be in a wheelchair in the next five years."

What? I'm strong. I'm healthy. I'm only in my thirties. This can't be my answer!

Determined to overcome this diagnosis, I began a regimen of prescribed medications, some of them experimental. After several months, I thought, *I should be feeling better by now,* but I wasn't. I was still struggling to keep moving every day, and my breathing had become labored.

On my best days, I huffed and puffed like an 80-year-old man who'd smoked every day of his adult life, and believe me, I'd never been a smoker.

As my breathing continued to decline, I was referred to a pulmonologist. I was frustrated. *Seriously, two specialists in a few months' time? I didn't even want to go to the first doctor.*

It turned out to be a good thing. The pulmonologist discovered that some of the medications I was taking were affecting my breathing. I immediately stopped taking the medications and was now under the care of a pulmonologist and had a chest scan every few months.

I thought it was funny to joke with Laura using a little play on words from the 1990 movie *Kindergarten Cop.* Before and after tests I would say, "It's a toomah!" If you don't know what I'm talking about, hop on YouTube and watch the *"It's NOT a toomah"* clip from the movie.

I'm sure she found my humor quite juvenile and felt every bit as irritated as Arnold Schwarzenegger's character in the movie. She would fuss at me and say, "It's not funny! If you keep saying that, one of these days, it's gonna be a tumor!"

Coughing had become a way of life, but I was shocked when I coughed up blood on my drive home from work in August of 2003. If Laura had her way, I would have gone to the emergency room that night. I figured, *this is just another medication issue*, and waited to call my doctor the next morning.

He immediately ordered another scan. I went in for the test and was certain it would be clean as all the others had been.

Early the next morning, the doctor called. "Todd, I need to speak with Laura and you regarding your test results."

"Okay, Laura and I can come by after work today." I was surprised but not alarmed at this point.

"No, I need you to come immediately." Now the doctor's words had my attention.

This had never happened before. Feeling a bit nervous, I called Laura right away and quipped, "It's a tumor!"

Let's just say that didn't go over well. Maybe it was my delivery.

Laura and I hurried to meet at the doctor's office. There was no paperwork waiting to be filled out, and no hours wasted in a waiting room. We were barely there a minute when we were brought directly back to the doctor's private office where he sat behind a big oak desk waiting for us.

This was feeling more serious by the moment. The doctor walked over to his "thing on the wall" and switched on the first light.

"I have something I'd like to show you," the doctor shared. "Todd, this is your scan from last May. As you can see, it is clear."

As he switched on the next light, he indicated, "This is your scan from last night."

Laura and I stared at the two scans side by side. The second scan showed a large mass right next to my heart. We were speechless. And honestly, Laura was a little bit mad I had talked myself into having a tumor.

The doctor attempted to reassure us with a plan of action, "You will need to see a surgeon immediately. My office has set up an appointment for you." But the serious look of concern on his face told a different story.

After a few rounds with the insurance company, we finally met with the surgeon who immediately scheduled a biopsy.

By the end of the month, the biopsy procedure began in a hospital operating room, while Laura was surrounded by family and friends in the waiting room. Pastors from our church prayed with the family and began to sing hymns with Laura and our moms who had both come as soon as they heard the news. The beautiful lyrics of old-time hymns filled the waiting room.

> *"Then sings my soul, my Savior God, to Thee,*
> *how great Thou art," and "What can make me*
> *whole again? Nothing but the blood of Jesus."*

If you are familiar with these hymns, I hope you can hear them right now, followed by

> *"When peace like a river attendeth my soul,*
> *When sorrows like sea billows roll,*
> *Whatever my lot, thou hast taught me to say,*
> *It is well, it is well, with my soul."*

Only fifteen minutes into what was expected to be a two-hour long surgery, the surgeon walked in and cleared his throat.

"Mrs. Shoemaker, may I speak with you in the hall?"

Laura followed him into the hallway as the small crowd continued to sing.

"Mrs. Shoemaker, we have already discovered that the tumor is cancerous, and it is the size of a golf ball."

The sounds of the hymn faded into the distance and Laura was shook by this devastating news.

Soon after, we learned that I had thymus cancer and the doctors began discussing *the options* with us. Our choices included chemotherapy, radiation, or surgery to remove my thymus.

As I lay in ICU later that night, alone for the first time, I talked to God about my options. Except for the hum of machines, the room was quiet, and I listened for my answers.

"Todd, this is why I asked you to fast in New York City. I was preparing you for this moment, for a crazy, beautiful journey that will be a mystery to doctors, but I promise to be with you every step of the way. Yours will be a story that will encourage others for years to come."

I thanked God for his goodness, as I was already amazed at His plan. Without the arthritis diagnosis, I wouldn't have been on medication that affected my breathing and this cancer may not have been discovered early enough to successfully treat it.

You know what stood out to me most during my hospital stay – the smells. To this day, that smell is a reminder of God's promise to me. What started out as an act of obedience has become an amazing story. This was just the beginning; I had no idea at the time just how often I would be in hospitals.

As I researched and considered my options, I felt led to choose surgery. It was a good option because the tumor had been found early but presented challenges. The tumor could break apart during the procedure and spread the cancer to other parts of my body. My chest would have to be cracked open, as in open-heart surgery, making this a major procedure requiring months of recovery time.

After discussing this with Laura and my doctors, surgery was scheduled. On Tuesday, October 13, 2003, we stepped out of our home before the break of dawn and headed to the hospital.

As I'm sure most of you know, we arrived and we waited, and waited, for the procedure to begin. Imagine our surprise when as we sat waiting, there was a loud pop and we were surrounded in inky blackness. Just as I was beginning to wonder, *Is God trying to tell us something?* the generator kicked in and the fluorescent lights flickered back on.

Our pastors, Nathan and Andrew, who were there for moral support had a good time laughing with me about it. "What if that happens during the surgery!?!" we quipped.

Again, as I was wheeled into surgery, Laura was supported by family and friends in the waiting room. Our moms were with us for support during and after the surgery. To say that we felt well-loved would be an understatement.

Before surgery, the doctors had forewarned us I could be several hours in Post Op. Within minutes, I was asking questions in recovery. The nurses were dumbfounded! I shared that our friends and family had been praying for us and the medical staff.

The surgery was a success! Every bit of the tumor was removed, and the doctors declared me cancer-free!

The doctors also prepared us for months of recovery after the surgery. I was released a few days later on a sunny Saturday morning. Imagine how shocked Laura was as we prepared to leave the hospital and I declared, "Honey, I'm going to run marathons."

"Trust God from the bottom of your heart;
don't try to figure out everything on your own.
Listen for God 's voice in everything you do, everywhere
you go; he's the one who will keep you on track."
Proverbs 3: 5-6

Laura's Story

For me, this was an unsettling time. While Todd and the pastors were laughing when the lights went out, I was panicking. It was everything I could do just to remember to breathe, and then remember to pray. I felt as though I had been plunged into darkness and I was struggling to find my way.

I had only been married to my amazing man for four short years, and I was terrified I was going to lose him already. I had never been faced with the possible loss of a loved one, or even a life-threatening illness. It was incredibly different from anything I had dealt with before, and it presented a real challenge to my faith.

The day I sat in a chair across the desk from my soulmate's doctor and realized my love had a tumor, my faith was shattered. I was shocked; I was numb; I could barely process the bad news. I cried, and then cried some more.

It was the only way I could cope at the time because I knew full well that many good, Godly people went to heaven at an early age, but I was not ready to face a loss of this proportion. I thought to myself, *even mothers must survive the loss of their innocent babies. This could happen to me.*

I cried some more and prayed. *Lord, I don't understand the reasons you allow us to love and lose those who are precious to us. I don't want to be that person.* I begged, *Lord, please spare Todd and deliver his body from this tumor.*

The biopsy was scheduled quickly as the tumor seemed to be growing fast, from nothing in May to what we later learned was the size of a golf ball. The day of the biopsy was an absolute blur to me.

I was anchored in the comfort of our moms, our family, and friends. Even our pastors came to pray and sing hymns with us, but there was only one thing I wanted to hear. I kept thinking to myself, *the doctor is going to come out here and tell me we can put this scare behind us, and we could go on our merry way, happy and healthy, growing old together.*

Everything around me faded except the words of the surgeon, when he called me in the hall and told me that my husband, the man I was dreaming of growing old with, had cancer. Suddenly, there was barely time to think.

Life was a whirlwind. Options were discussed, challenges faced, prayers prayed, and within weeks we were facing major surgery to remove the cancerous tumor from Todd's chest. I cringed inside as the surgeon shared, "We will have to use a saw to cut through

Todd's rib cage."

I felt like I was lost in a strange country. I had never been here before, and I didn't want to be here now.

And then I was found – the tumor was successfully removed, and my love was declared cancer-free! Our future was suddenly restored. Relief washed away my fears like a warm shower soothing my aching soul. I could exhale and imagine us growing old together again.

When Todd boldly announced, "Honey, I'm going to run marathons!" I smiled lovingly into his eyes and said, "Honey, whatever you want to do, but no more tumors!"

We had no idea what the next challenges would be, but I wanted Todd to do whatever made him happy. We had a second chance at life, and as far as I was concerned if it wasn't a tumor, it was a free-for-all, an adventure. We had faced the possibility of life being over, and the number ONE priority on my agenda was to enjoy life to the fullest!

1/2

Little did I know, this was the beginning of a seventeen-year crazy, beautiful journey with the love of my life, my soulmate, and best friend. Our fight for life, for love, for every moment has taught us to find joy in the suffering, and trust that "all things work together for good for those that love God and are called to His Purpose."

SHOEMAKER

Chapter Three

A Steadfast Race

Hebrews 12:1-3

"Honey, I'm gonna run marathons!"

Imagine my wife's surprise at my startling declaration, "Honey, I'm gonna run marathons!"

Her eyebrows raised, her brow crinkled, and she cocked her head to the side with eyes wide and asked hesitantly, "Todd, have you ever run a marathon?"

I shook my head no, she took a deep breath and patiently responded, "When is the last time you actually ran?"

I thought about it for a moment and remembered my running days shortly after high school, nearly twenty years ago, and before I could answer out loud, my beautiful wife smiled and said, "You know what? Go for it!!"

And so, I did! After twenty years of not running at all, after five months of healing from major surgery, I started running. And what a sight I was!

Let me tell you, I had no clue how to train for a marathon, and much to my dismay I did not look like one of those graceful runners you see gliding down the road from time to time. But I knew God was giving me a story to tell, and I believed He wanted me to start running, so I said, "Yes."

I went to one of those fancy running stores where they fit you for just the right shoes. I sought the company of other runners and listened to their advice. I read everything I could get my hands on about *HOW* to run a marathon. I didn't always listen to the advice, or heed what I'd learned, but I didn't give up!

I kept on running! I kept on training! I truly believed that when we allow God to lead us, we can accomplish great things!

And on November 14, 2004, I did it! Well, I half-way did it!!

I crossed the finish line on my first half marathon! I wasn't even sure I would finish, but my beautiful bride was beaming at me from the sidelines when I crossed the finish line.

As I ran the race, I crossed paths with a young lady. She would run past me, I would pass her, back and forth we went until eventually we were running side by side. We chatted a bit as we ran, and I learned she was a trauma nurse.

"This will be my last race for a while," she shared. The reason why was obvious. She was very pregnant.

She smiled and rubbed her bump in the way expectant mothers often do. "This little one will arrive in about a month."

"Wow!" I was impressed, and I was even more impressed when she beat my time by one second.

So, yeah, when I ran my first race, I got beat by an eight-month pregnant nurse! But I wasn't giving up, I was already half-way there, and I was determined to meet the challenge of a full marathon.

After the race, I was plagued with fatigue and incredibly tired. I'd been training and preparing for months and chalked it up to all the hard work. I had read that some participants collapse after a race, and honestly, just thought the way I was feeling was a part of running I'd have to get used to.

A couple of weeks after the race, I collapsed at home. I could barely move and was kind of delirious, but I somehow managed to call Laura at work.

As soon as she answered the phone, she knew something was seriously wrong. "Todd, what's happening? Are you sick again?" she asked in a panic.

Even in her worry and fear, my love manages to stay level-headed in a crisis. She called an ambulance from another line while she kept me on the phone. The paramedics soon arrived and immediately rushed me to the hospital. Laura hurried to meet us there. I was quickly admitted and spent Thanksgiving week in the hospital. This was the first of many holidays I would spend in the hospital.

Let me give you a little advice — if you ever find yourself in the hospital on Thanksgiving, don't trust the holiday meal delivered to your room!

During my hospital stay, I was diagnosed with Myasthenia Gravis, an incurable disease which affects the muscles. My first thought was, *Oh great! I'm halfway to running a marathon. Is this disease going to take that away?*

As often happens with a new medical diagnosis, I was referred to a specialist for more tests.

We traveled to Miami, Florida, to meet with my newest doctor. He poked and prodded and did all the things doctors do before starting the conversation, "Let's talk about how this diagnosis might affect your life."

This was the moment I'd been dreading.

Laura jumped in and excitedly shared, "Well, less than a month ago Todd completed his first half marathon."

"What?!?" the doctor exclaimed, "That is not possible. There is no way you could have MG and be running."

The diagnosis was called into question, and I couldn't have been happier. "Does this mean I can keep running?" I blurted out.

I didn't know it at the time, but this would become a question I often asked of medical professionals.

"I don't see why not," the doctor responded, "If you were running before, go for it." This was my second *go for it*, and that's exactly what I planned to do.

I took a short break, a few weeks, and then I put *my boogie on* (aka running shoes) and started running again.

The New Year started with a bang on January 1, 2008. I woke up that day and heard God speak to me, *Todd, I need you to run a thousand miles.* Yup, you read that right! No big deal, right? That's only about 38 marathons in a year, one every 9 days. Seemed do-able to me!

At this point, I had been diagnosed with Young Onset Parkinson's and my body was just not the same. Despite that, I stepped up (no pun intended) to the challenge!

As always, so did my wonderful, supportive, loving wife! By now, she was used to me challenging myself, my doctor didn't object, and Laura smiled her sweet smile and said, "Honey, whatever makes you happy."

I started my journey of 1,000 miles, and let me tell you my spirit was willing, but my body was not very enthused with this new adventure. I went through pair after pair of running shoes racking up the miles. I started to notice my times were getting slower. Let's face it, I had never been fast, but I'd also never been soooooooo slow.

It didn't matter that I was slow, when it came to long distance running, I could run forever... well it seemed like forever. As my Parkinson's progressed, sleep had become an issue for me, so I would get up at two or three in the morning and go running for hours. And when I say hours, I mean hours! Think five hours at a time! The way I saw it if I couldn't sleep, I might as well go running. Stride after stride brought me closer and closer to the 1,000-mile mark. I loved every minute of it!

I've often been asked, "When God asks you to do these things, do you actually hear an audible voice?" The answer is *no*. Yet there have been numerous occasions where my spirit has been aware of God speaking to me. Remember the fast?

That's what I loved about my middle-of-the-night marathons. It was just God and me, not another soul on the road, and we had some great conversations. It was my time with Him, time to pray, and to seek guidance. Time to hear His voice as He challenged and encouraged me.

Except one night… when there was something else on the road, and it was not another human! While I was enjoying my 2 a.m. run, I noticed something crossing at the street light about 20 feet in front of me. I chuckled to myself as I thought, *Hmmm, crossing at the light… that seems like a responsible decision.* Suddenly I remembered what you may already be thinking, *Todd, you are not fast!*

And I began to pray in earnest, *Lord, please don't let them look my way!*

That night, it was just God, two coyotes, and me, with only open road between us! My prayers must have been working; they didn't even glance my way. I took off running at a pace I didn't know I was capable of any longer. I made it home in record time that morning. Who knows, maybe I could have made the Olympic sprint team, but that is not what God had called me to do.

Running 26.2 miles beside thousands of other humans gave me an opportunity to share God's story with others who, ordinarily, may have never looked to me for encouragement. Being slow gave me the advantage of having lots of time to talk. Conversations generally started with, "So, why are you running today?"

There were so many reasons - "My mom is fighting for her life." "My father had a heart attack." "My child has been diagnosed with a rare illness." "A cousin/friend/sister… (you fill in the blanks.)"

You see, this was never about me. It was about the story God was giving me… it was about the strength He was giving me… it was about His faithfulness in all He was bringing me through… it was about running for those who couldn't run for themselves!

I proudly bore the names of those I was running for on the shirts

Laura lovingly made for race days. Each shirt was covered in names of those who couldn't physically run for themselves; one of those names was my wonderful mother-in-law.

Many people have travelled through challenging times, and I was blessed to share God's encouragement with them, it was never rejected. My fellow runners, my fellow travelers, had open ears and open hearts.

The year 2008 flew by, the miles added up, and so did the challenges. My body screamed at me with every mile, but I was determined to reach the goal. In October 2008, as I was running and enjoying another midnight conversation with God, I felt Him tell me to enjoy running because soon I would be running a new race.

Cool, I thought, *I'm going to start training for triathlons.* I'd been considering that challenge for some time. I'd earned my 1,000-miles-in-one-year shirt. For real, been there, done that, got the t-shirt, and it was so worth it! I would be eligible to run in the New York marathon in 2011. I had plans to run across Florida to fight human trafficking. *Who knew,* I thought to myself, *I might even run across the country.* Let's just say I had *BIG* plans!!

Little did I know God was preparing me for a race I never would have chosen for myself – my body was fighting a battle that would change my life again. My story, God's story - a tale of overcoming, being encouraged, never giving up, facing a storm and coming through on the other side, and lessons learned – a story meant to be shared was continuing to unfold.

"I'm glad in God, far happier than you would ever guess - happy that you're again showing such strong concern for me. Not that you ever quit praying and thinking about me. You just had no chance to show it. Actually, I don't have a sense of needing

anything personally. I've learned by now to be quite content whatever my circumstances. I'm just as happy with little as with much, with much as with little. I've found the recipe for being happy whether full or hungry, hands full or hands empty. Whatever I have, wherever I am, I can make it through anything in the One who makes me who I am. I don't mean that your help didn't mean a lot to me - it did. It was a beautiful thing that you came alongside me in my troubles."
Philippians 4:10-13

Laura's Story

Oh! My! Goodness! Todd's first race was soooo exciting! I told everyone I knew about it! I invited every friend, every family member, maybe even a few strangers on the street!

Team Todd was my mission, and I take my missions very seriously, with a smile, of course. I recruited team members, designed and printed Team Todd replica racing "bibs" proudly displaying Todd's race number to wear on our t-shirts or to hold up as signs. I was determined that my amazing husband would have the best support system known to man.

And it worked! On race day, everyone was there! His mom, his aunts, his brother, our friends, and maybe even a few strangers I'd recruited along the way.

Have I mentioned it was exciting? This was Todd's first official race; the big day that he'd been training for. Todd ran 25-33 miles several times a week in preparation for this race. I was even interviewed by the local news before the race, right at the start line.

I was giddy, like a schoolgirl, as I waited to cheer my sweetheart on, surrounded by Team Todd, every member eager to cheer for our hero.

We arrived early, before the crack of dawn, at 4:30 a.m. The day started out cool and refreshing as the anticipation along with the sun rose over the horizon above the island of Palm Beach.

The morning went on and my excitement grew as I waited for my love to cross the finish line. I thought back to that day in the hospital when Todd proclaimed that he was going to run marathons. I believed it, but I could barely believe it. We had come through a major health scare; what seemed like just a short time ago, I had been afraid I might lose the love of my life. But here we were, collecting another life experience together. It was an experience I will never forget!!

There was more training and there were more races. I would wake up in the morning to a quiet house and know Todd was out training. It warmed my heart to know he was thriving in his element, spending time with God, but I also missed his early morning wake-up songs. I am not an early riser, and my sweetheart's wonderful voice would wake me with songs personalized just for me.

Not only did I miss Todd's singing, but I worried a bit, too. Todd is a creature of habit which means I knew his regular route and where to find him if he didn't return in a timely manner. There were mornings when Todd would become so exhausted, he couldn't run another step, and he would call for help. This means there were mornings of panic (yes, I'm still human), and my mind would sometimes torment me with frightening thoughts. *Is the cancer back? Is this the end? Will I be a widow, after all?*

While many of Todd's races are amongst my fondest memories, there is one race, the Disney race, that has burned not-so-fond memories in my mind. I waited and waited at the finish line, in the hot sun, for over six hours! I hoped and prayed he was safe, and not with the paramedics somewhere in the Magic Kingdom. I paced, and prayed, and prayed some more, until finally I saw a man who resembled Todd, walking, slowly, barely.

I held my breath, watched, and waited, until I realized the sickly-looking man, pale as a ghost, was Todd. My heart ached; I wanted to scream and cry, to grab him and snatch him from what looked like death's grip. I held in my fears and moaned in my spirit, *please God, please let this be his last race. This is killing him.*

This was Todd's last marathon and to this day I regret what I wished for. I knew how passionate he was about running. I knew it was like breathing for him. He had to do it! But in that moment, he was too close to death for my comfort, and I was not ready to give him up freely.

Please don't confuse this for a lack of trust in God for my husband's well-being. I trusted, but I had also witnessed the death of good people. I knew Christian women who were faced with the reality of widowhood at a young age. It wasn't because there was some hidden sin in their life, or that they were not worthy of being healed. God loves each and every one, but none of us is exempt to the reality of death, even when we are young. This drives me to love more, argue less, praise God for every blessing, and be present in the moments.

When I look back at this memorable time, I realize it was just the beginning of a journey I couldn't even imagine. God had big plans for us, and my Christian walk was about to take a detour – a meander that would grow my trust in the Lord in a way I couldn't yet begin to fathom.

SHOEMAKER

Chapter Four

The Family Fiasco

"Mom, you set my head on fire!"

Let me take you back to the beginning of our Family Fiasco. Well, it probably started long before the day I left the hospital after surgery... but THAT day was quite an adventure.

It was the first time I had been outside in days. I was enjoying the ride home with the sun warming my skin and beautiful blue skies above. The fresh air outside of the hospital was wonderful except... I was riding in a car hugging a teddy bear (to protect my sutures) with three anxious women: my beautiful wife who was driving 20 mph, and both of our dangerously nurturing mothers.

The noise was overwhelming. Laura blew the horn every time a car came anywhere near ours.

"Todd are you okay?" my mom repeated every few seconds. Laura's mom was praying out loud during all this. And I was thinking, *I can't wait to be home resting in my recliner!*

Let me add that we went to church that evening, and repeated this fiasco, again, which brings me to our wonderful church family at the time. For a month after my surgery, they became the hands and feet of Jesus and helped us in many ways. With Laura working full time, and the moms there to look after me, we really appreciated the daily meal deliveries.

And then, there were more. More meals, more desserts, more food than we could possibly eat! When I say desserts, what I really mean is brownies! Imagine a daily brownie delivery, right to your front door! Really, who doesn't love brownies? I'll tell you who, people who have them every day for a month!

Lest I sound ungrateful, let me assure you, Laura and I have the fondest memories of those days, but we both found it difficult to even look at a brownie for years.

Laura and I were not only blessed with a great church family, we were also blessed with great moms. As soon as our moms found out about my biopsy, Laura's mom picked up my mom and headed to West Palm Beach, Florida to take care of "their babies." They were there whenever we needed them, and we never had to ask.

One day we expected them at our place in the late morning, definitely by lunchtime. Lunch came and went, with no sign of our dynamic duo. Remember, this was 2003, back in the day when not everyone had a cell phone. We were frantic with worry all day!

Finally, as the sun was setting, our moms came careening in the driveway. As they walked through the front door, both Laura and I pointed out the time and asked sternly, "Where have you been?!?"

Our moms laughed and giggled without a care in the world. "We decided to stop for lunch...," my mom began.

"... and then we decided to explore a little bit." added Laura's mom.

Laura and I looked at each other incredulously.

"When we finally got back in the car, I was helping with directions...," my mom shared sheepishly.

Now Laura and I were really craning our necks at each other. *My mom hadn't driven a day in her life, and she was the one directing.*

Laura's mom hooted and added, "It's okay. We were only about an hour north before I realized we were heading the wrong way." They bumped shoulders and giggled some more!

By this time Laura and I were laughing with them, relieved that they were at our house and not somewhere in Georgia.

The laughing and giggling didn't stop the whole time they were with us. Laura would have to get out of bed at night and ask, "Can you two quiet down some so we could get some sleep?"

It was great to have our moms with us. It has given us great content for this book! LOL! Boy, do we have some adventures to share with you.

Laura's mom had to return home to Dade City, Florida after a few weeks, and my mom decided to stay a while longer. She pushed herself to her limits taking care of Laura, and me, her baby. One day she was especially tired, and thought she'd get ahead of the game by warming up dinner before Laura returned home from work.

She chose from the myriad of Tupperware full of food in our fridge and placed it in the oven. You read that right! Of course, it wasn't long after that our entire home was engulfed in what I believe must be one of the worst smells known to mankind. Mom accidentally warmed a Tupperware container full of lasagna in our oven. Can you imagine the delicious ooey-gooey lasagna, and plastic, dripping down to the bottom of our oven?

We were thanking God the house didn't catch fire that day, I was too sore to run! We were especially thankful we had more food, and brownies.

Our moms were the best of friends. They were in their element, taking care of the two of us, and having the time of their lives. They got to do it again, a month later, when I had open-heart surgery to remove the tumor. They enjoyed another fun, laughter and tear-filled trip to West Palm Beach together. I am happy to report they managed to find their way safely and on time, much to both Laura's and my relief.

Again, what should have been an everyday occurrence turned into a fiasco. Let me explain; after open-heart surgery to remove my tumor, showering became a difficult task for me, well, let's say for all of us.

Even the warmest shower left me shivering and shaking uncontrollably. As you can guess, this is not a good thing after your chest has been cracked open.

I would shower, and Laura and the moms would cry and pray. Me, I screamed and cried in pain. What a sight we all must have been!! Can't you just picture this on a reality TV show? Believe it or not, it gets better!

One night my mom shared a fantastic solution to our problem, "I can put a towel in the dryer while Todd showers, and when he gets out, Laura can wrap him up in the warmed towel." This sounded like a great plan to all of us.

Let's just say the execution of that idea did not go as planned! It went something like this. Laura helps me take a shower. Shower ends. Mom has towel warmed and ready to go. Laura reaches through the bathroom door and quickly grabs said towel. Laura throws the towel, as fast as she can over my head. The plan is working! Wait, my head is on fire! You read that right!

"Mom, you set my head on fire!!" I yelled.

Lucky for me, I was rocking the bald look, and had no hair to burn off! As you can imagine, there were more tears after this incident.

My poor mom was so sleep-deprived and concerned about me, she accidentally put the dry towel, not in the dryer, but in the microwave to warm it. The towel was literally on fire when Laura tossed it over my head!

Laura and I still have the burnt towel as a memento of all this mom love. We are not sure how we survived it to this day! And yet, we couldn't, and wouldn't have done it without them.

We, too soon, learned what it would be like to live without one of our mothers. Laura's mom went home to be with Jesus in 2006. Barely a day goes by that we don't think about her, talk about her, remember her fondly.

Let me tell you about Laura's mom. I fell in love with Mom West the first time I met her, all the way back in 1999. She was one of those people who are incredibly easy to love. She was absolutely authentic; there was nothing fake about her. She loved fiercely - her family, her friends, anyone God brought into her life, including a young man who wanted to marry her daughter, after only a few short months.

I often joke with Laura, "You know your mom sealed the deal, right?"

Seriously, I can't imagine who wouldn't have wanted to be her son-in-law! Of course, she never treated me like an "in-law," she treated me like family. From day one, I was her son.

A year after my cancer diagnosis, she was diagnosed with lung cancer. Her diagnosis shook the family to its core. *She did everything right. She ate healthy food. She worked out. She hadn't smoked a day in her life. How could this happen to her!?!*

Her doctors gave her a year, but let me tell you, Mom West was a fighter! She was encouraged by my running and I was inspired by her will to live. Both of our lives had been interrupted by cancer, and we were kindred spirits!

My running filled Mom West with so much hope that I would train on the track outside her hospital window. Her words, "Todd, every time I see you run, I am filled with a deep desire to join you someday," encouraged me.

Every time I rounded a lap, looked up and saw her watching through the window, I hoped for the same.

Mom West loved sunflowers; every year she lovingly cultivated them in her backyard. Laura created a prayer quilt covered in sunflowers, and we gifted her with the brightest yellow running shoes you've ever seen. Just as yellow symbolizes hope, we hoped with the brightest of hopes.

She pressed on and fought cancer for two years, long past doctor's predictions, before she lost her courageous battle. She is missed by many every day!

The medical world cannot put a timeframe on someone's heart or their desire to live. Momma West was determined to beat cancer and run with me. God answered our prayers; just in a different way than we had hoped. She is completely healed, dancing and rejoicing with Jesus. Maybe they even run laps on streets of gold.

*"Anyone who meets a testing challenge head-on
and manages to stick it out is mighty fortunate.
For such persons loyally in love with God,
the reward is life and more life."*
James 1:12

Laura's Story

I lovingly refer to this time as The Mom Invasion. Imagine scary music playing...

Let me paint a picture of our home and life at the time. We were in a 2-bedroom, 2-bath apartment with two unruly and rambunctious basset hound puppies. When our moms finally arrived, the puppies were quite jealous. They liked attention, and lots of it!

Lulu, our problem child, would see my mom on the couch, run full-throttle across the living room and take a flying leap into her lap at just the right moment – when mom was taking a sip of coffee. You can imagine what happened, coffee everywhere.

You see it wasn't just the moms and us; it was the moms, and the puppies, and the visitors, and us. You get the idea!

I am so glad Todd is a strong man! He needed to be to survive his "caregivers" after surgery.

What a sight we were! Todd in his wheelchair, chest glued together, the giggly moms, the crazy pups, and capable me.

I was attentive to Todd's every need. Once I saw a pesky mosquito flying around my sweetheart. That creature had the nerve to land right on his chest. Don't worry, I took care of that!

Stress and sleep-deprivation weren't going to slow me down. I slapped that sucker as hard as I could. Suddenly, I was awake. The annoying buzz of the mosquito came to an end, and the room was filled with silence, as I realized with a jolt what I had just done. Todd sat there in shock, and pain, lots of pain.

I couldn't even look at him, I was so terrified. I looked at our moms in a panic. "Did I just break him?"

Todd wasn't broken, and I was forgiven, grateful he still loved me! I'm still surprised to this day that all of us survived the many unfortunate blunders of our family fiasco.

But let me be clear, I could not have made it through Todd's surgery and recovery without our moms, and I could not be more grateful for the love and nurture we received from them, the friendship they shared with each other, and the fun they brought to this time of our lives.

Just before I learned of my sweet momma's Stage 4 lung cancer, I started grad School. I was devastated by the news!

The two best people I knew had now been diagnosed with cancer. Their strong faith in the Lord, along with their excellent character, had been a source of love for each other from the start. This new battle only served to draw them closer.

During mom's first hospital stay, Todd was a constant source of inspiration. Even though surgery was unsuccessful, and the huge cancerous tumor could not be removed from her lung, she found the strength and faith. Mom believed God would bring her through this journey, just as she had seen Him do for Todd.

There were shade trees and a path just outside her hospital window. She was filled with hope as she sat at the window and watched Todd run. Her faith was strengthened as she witnessed Todd running toward God's will for his life! She envisioned her life leading down the same path.

What a blessing it was to witness my two-favorite people in the world, my rocks, inspire each other through God's grace and glory! These memorable moments will forever be dear to my heart.

When I look back on that time, I believe God orchestrated the start of my graduate program at just the right time. It was the perfect distraction from all that was happening in my life. I was working full time, supporting Todd through his many hospital and doctor visits, and my school work kept me focused.

I lived in Palm Beach County, Florida; mom lived in Dade City, a small town near Tampa, Florida. I wanted to spend as much time as possible with my mom, but I knew that finishing my graduate degree would make her proud. I was driven to succeed, for mom, and God gave me the strength to carry on.

SHOEMAKER

Chapter Five

Becoming an Abolitionist

"If I had the time... I'd fight this crime!"

Have you ever wondered what inspires a person to write a book? Let me tell you about when I first thought of writing a book.

While I was still running, I was blessed with the opportunity to share my story at several churches and schools. I love to share my story, to encourage others to live out their God-given dreams, and to remind the world, "Never allow the storms of life to steal your hopes and dreams. Every one of us has a story to share."

Not only has God given me a story, He continues to strengthen me as I live it out. I am energized when I share, I truly enjoy the interactions, and love giving credit to the One who makes it all possible.

Funny thing about stories, especially our life stories – they are always moving and changing and becoming more. I survived a fast in New York City, a tumor, major surgery, and running 1,000 miles in a year when my story took another unexpected turn.

In 2006, Laura and I were out for a run. Well, I was running. Laura followed me on her bike.

"Honey, why don't you move your right arm when you run?" she hollered from behind.

I stopped, bent over and took a deep breath, looked back at her and asked, "What are you talking about?"

Looking thoughtful, Laura made a request, "Just walk ahead of me for a minute or two."

As I walked, I thought to myself, *Hmmm, I've never noticed that before.*

"Sweetheart, you're right, my arm isn't moving when I walk."

We finished our run and headed home. At Laura's insistence, we scheduled an appointment with my neurologist the next day. After a year of test after test to rule out a multitude of illnesses, there was one diagnosis that popped up repeatedly. The doctors insisted I was too young. Yet, in September 2007, as my symptoms worsened, I was officially diagnosed with Young Onset Parkinson's. I was only 41.

As you might be able to guess, my first question for the doctor was, "Can I continue to run?"

"As long as your body allows it, keep running," the doctor encouraged.

Over time, I lost the natural swing in both arms. It made running more of a challenge, but it didn't stop me.

A diagnosis of Young Onset Parkinson's was monumental, and I wondered what I could do to mark this moment in my life. I had always wanted to go skydiving and decided this presented the perfect opportunity.

You may be asking, "Why would anyone want to jump out of a perfectly good airplane?"

I'd heard that question often, but it seemed to me it would be an amazing experience, and it was.

On a cool November morning, we arrived early and eager, filled out the necessary forms, watched the mandatory instructional video, and boarded a perfectly good plane with the intention of jumping out.

As the plane made its ascent, and the land below became smaller and smaller, I was suddenly filled with fear – *Is this really such a good idea? Can I jump out of a plane? After all I've survived, is this worth the risk?*

Fear did not win this war! After all, I am an overcomer! I knew I would regret it if I tapped out!

At 14,000 feet, strapped to my instructor, he turned to me and yelled, "Do you want to keep it simple or do some flips on the way down?"

I didn't hesitate to look him in the eye and declare, "Let's flip." If I was going to do this, I was going all the way.

And then, we took the leap! In reality, we kneeled at the edge of the door, and flipped out of a moving airplane. What a thrill! The view was breathtaking, and the experience was amazing. I loved every minute of my adventure.

Before I knew it, we landed safely. As always, my beautiful wife was there waiting for me with a big smile on her face. I'm sure there was a little relief mixed in with her smile.

Since that time, I have become active in finding a cure for Young Onset Parkinson's. I'm working to educate others regarding the disease and writing letters to politicians encouraging funding. I am optimistic and hopeful that one day a cure will be found.

Many people are aware of Parkinson's thanks to Michael J. Fox and Muhammad Ali, and believe it is about tremors, but this disease involves a huge umbrella of symptoms. Every patient presents differently. My symptoms include rigidity, slowness of movement, and it affects my cognitive skills. The symptoms have worsened through the years, and I do experience minor tremors.

I've also become actively involved in the fight against human trafficking. My first exposure to this crime was through Law & Order. At first, I thought, *it's just a TV show, and surely this doesn't happen in America,* but the researcher in me began to investigate. I was shocked and broken-hearted to realize not only was human trafficking happening in America, it was happening in my own backyard.

It wasn't enough to simply realize this was happening, I had a deep desire to do something about it, to help in some way. Laura and I had countless conversations and I shared with her, "If I had the time, I'd fight this crime... full time, and I'd do it for free."

She encouraged me, "Pray about it, you never know when God will open a door to a new opportunity."

As my illness progressed, I continued to work full-time. I was not ready to retire, yet. I was only 42 years old. My resistance to change was making my life worse. I would work for a few days and end up in the hospital for weeks.

Finally, during one hospital stay, the doctor sat down next to me, looked at me seriously, and said, "Todd, it's time to retire. Work can no longer be a part of your life, if you want to maintain any quality of life."

As I sat, devastated, after the doctor left the room, I sensed God speaking to my heart, again. *Todd, remember what you told Laura a few years ago? I am giving you the time to join the fight to end human trafficking.* What looked like the end, was actually a new beginning. I reminded myself, *God is always on time.*

The church I was attending at the time invited me to join a group of individuals who wanted to discuss how we could fight this crime and educate others about it. Throughout these discussions the ministry, Hope for Freedom, was born. Hope for Freedom succeeded in its mission and is now in the Palm Beach County School District educating students and staff regarding the dangers of human trafficking.

If you know someone who needs help, please call the Human Trafficking Hotline number 1-888-373-7888.

Since 2009, I have been blessed with the opportunity to help several organizations fight this crime and educate the public through social media. I am grateful, to this day, that I followed my heart, listened to God, and took on this challenge.

Not only had my working days come to an end, but in March 2009, my running days also came to an end. I had pushed my body to its limits and on a Friday night, Laura rushed me to the emergency room where the doctors quickly pulled her aside and admonished, "It's time to put your husband's affairs in order."

I was not expected to make it through the weekend, but after 20 days in the hospital I made a recovery, was released, and sent home. This routine of illness and grueling hospital stays became our new normal in 2009.

This was not an easy time. When I was told I would not be able to run again, I felt a small part of me die. Marathon season is a sad time for me, and even after all these years, I still miss running!

I mourned the loss of my health, my work, and my ability to run, but God opened door after door. For every loss, there was a blessing. God prepared me every step of the way for each challenge. From the fast in New York City, to having cancer. From telling me I would be running a different race soon, to the Parkinson's diagnosis.

Just imagine; God even turned doctor appointments and hospital stays into a mission field for me. At my local hospital, there is evidence of my prayers for the other patients in the form of a groove on the 4th floor. This groove is a symbol of hope, of a God who shows up in even the most difficult situations. It is also evidence of my new normal. I still run a race, at a much slower pace, but I will still finish strong.

"Learn to do good. Work for justice. Help the down-and-out. Stand up for the homeless. Go to bat for the defenseless. Let's Argue this out."
Isaiah 1:17

Laura's Story

I can remember that exciting weekend when we decided to skydive. It was the spur of the moment, on a beautiful clear day. The hues of blue skies were so brilliant and exhilarating without a cloud in sight.

We were so excited to skydive together! It would be another memorable event to check off our bucket list. I told myself, "I got this."

After all, I had a blast when I parasailed over the ocean with my former roommate, looking down on all the high-rise condominiums, that appeared so small. I loved the experience and I loved heights!

When we arrived, the airplane hangar was buzzing with activities as staff spread out multi-color parachutes. The floor of the hangar was bright and festive with a rainbow of color. I was mesmerized with the meticulous preparations and safety measures staff took to carefully fold and pack these beautiful parachutes.

We must have waited 45-60 minutes to go up in the air, waiting for the previous skydivers to complete their jump and staff regroup. During this time, my excitement began to fade and shriveled to doubt, lots of doubt.

Before we signed our contract and made payment, I had changed my mind. I chickened out! I backed down! I had way too many butterflies in my stomach to be enthusiastic as I thought I was about this adventure.

When I finally decided I would not "make the plunge", such relief came over me and I felt myself exhale. Now I could relax. So, I focused on Todd's memorable experience. I watched him practice with his tandem partner and get all suited up in his harness.

My excitement started to fade, again, watching him walk to that airplane. The butterflies that I had said goodbye to when I decided not to jump were now fluttering frantically in my stomach.

I watched the plane leave the ground and said a prayer. "Okay God, you brought him this far, bring him back to ground safely." My feet were safely planted on the ground, and gladly, as I eagerly watched the plane. Then he jumped!

He jumped! He actually did it. I searched for his parachute, so I could follow it. Wow! As they soar through the air, I glued my eyes to them and waited for him to land, and what a landing it was that day. It was perfect form, landing, walking, not even eating dust!

I was so elated he did it and that he finished it in one piece, I was jumping up and down cheering him on! It was truly an amazing moment.

The time during Todd's medical journey that led to full-time disability, was unsettling, but God was in the midst of the situation and continued to show us His grace, mercy and provisions. Going from two incomes to one was proof of it.

We were blessed during the ongoing financial and medical storm. God actually protected our marriage so that those challenges did not bring division in our relationship.

Trusting in the Lord became like oxygen, something we desperately needed. And He proved Himself faithful to provide for our needs. We came to a harsh reality that Todd would apply for Social Security Disability, at 42-years-old. So many folks forewarned us that we should brace ourselves for denied applications, multiple times. We did not find one person who was approved after the first application.

God brought to us a dear friend who knew how to apply and helped us complete the overwhelming process. Without her, we would have been one of the many initially denied. However, God blessed us and the process. Within 3 months of our initial application being submitted, we received a large deposit from the U.S. Government in our bank account, retroactive funds for the three months.

It was another reminder that God cared for us and knew our struggles. He provided for our physical and financial needs along with building our faith. This blessing also confirmed to me that Todd should fight human trafficking and do it for free.

I worked for the Palm Beach County School District as their first Foster Care Liaison and I learned so much from Todd and his research.

Serving children in foster care has been rewarding and challenging and I feel privileged to serve them. These children are at higher risk of being targeted by traffickers while in foster care, or in group homes, or when on the run.

Those youth who age out of foster care without support, are at higher risk of becoming homeless and vulnerable to believing the lies of traffickers, that they will "love and care" for them. In reality they become enslaved, usually before these young people realize what is happening.

It has been my honor for the past 8 years to serve this population through education. I pray for them, support them, and serve them. Isn't it amazing how God has weaved our passions together and allows Todd and me to serve and care about the same cause?

Chapter Six

The Sickly Support

"He lasted this long!"

In 2009, our crazy, beautiful journey took an unexpected turn, and as we navigated this new health journey, we were bombarded with information, and had more questions than we had answers.

I was concerned at the thought that I might not be able to uphold my portion of the 60-year contract I made with Laura on our wedding day. Emotions were running high, and I recalled all that Laura's father had endured when our beloved Momma West passed away in 2006.

There were no arrangements. She passed away on a Friday night, and on Saturday morning Laura's dad was at the funeral home trying to make important decisions in the midst of life-shattering grief. There were even family disputes regarding these important decisions.

I was certain I did not want my precious wife to have to face all the decisions alone or to experience family strife if God called me home. I talked to Laura and we made an appointment with the funeral home.

We spoke with the funeral director, took our time, and asked lots of questions. Now, all of our end-of-life decisions have been made and are in writing. It is our gift to each other and our loved ones.

Just as a conversation about funeral arrangements with your spouse can be awkward when faced with serious health issues, conversations with others can get a little odd, too.

The truth is when it comes to the "hard things," people just don't know what to say. They want to say something encouraging, or share words of comfort, but sometimes really crazy things come out instead.

In the early days, many of these comments bothered and even hurt Laura and me. Over the years we have learned to laugh and embrace our mutual love of dark humor.

A friend of ours once asked Laura, "How's Todd doing?"

"He's back in the hospital and not doing well," she shared.

Without missing a beat our friend replied, "Well, he has lasted this long." No words can express how that felt. We can laugh about it now, but at the time, Laura was devastated.

People often inquire regarding the health issues I am suffering from. Nine times out of ten, when Laura and I share my diagnosis, people respond with, "My Aunt So-and-So had the same thing and she passed away."

Really? Wow! Thanks for the encouraging word.

One of our all-time "favorites" is, "Todd, you must have a lot of sin in your life." Or how about that person who admonishes, "Todd, you just need to think more positive." And then there's the skeptic – "Todd, you don't look or act sick. Are you sure you're not faking it?" What?!?

When my health challenges changed my life in 2009, I asked God to help me never look or act sick, so this comment has become a cool opportunity to share God's love and blessing. Bet they didn't see that coming!

Don't forget the doctors who are concerned I am TOO positive. "Todd, it is quite common for patients in your position to experience depression. Are you sure you aren't depressed?"

Again, another chance to share how my faith in God and his faithfulness to me have kept me from dealing with depression and anger.

I'll let you in on a little secret... I am NOT Mr. Positive all the time. Every day is not smooth sailing on this journey. I have days that are incredibly tough, and I want to take a moment to encourage anyone who might be dealing with depression, anger, or thoughts of harming yourself, there is no shame in reaching out for help.

Call a friend or make an appointment with a professional if needed. If you are struggling with harmful thoughts, call the Suicide Hotline at 1-800-273-8255. Please don't suffer alone.

Everyone going through health challenges needs heathy support. Now that I've shared the mini-manual on what not to say, I'd like to share some practical tips for those wanting to offer support.

Be Present. Don't allow the busyness of life to distract you from the important things. When someone comes to spend time with me during treatments or my hospital stays, not only is it a blessing, but it is a gift that I treasure.

Ask Questions. Never be afraid to ask how it's going or admit you don't know how to help. I appreciate the opportunity to share what I need, rather than have someone guess what they should do or say.

Listen. Don't try to put yourself in my shoes. Just listen, on my good days and my bad days.

Be Specific. Don't offer, "Let me know what you need." Offer specific support that you know you can give. A meal, a ride to an appointment, a day of respite for a caregiver are all examples of specific support.

Follow Through. Those struggling with chronic illness feel like a burden at times, and a caregiver's plate can be so full that they will depend on the help you've offered to make it through the day. Even the smallest offers of support can be huge. Once you know how you can help, and offer specific support, make sure you do it. Don't make excuses or cancel at the last moment.

Be Flexible. Life with chronic illness is unpredictable. I may feel great one day and make plans with you, but once it arrives it may be a bad day for me. If I need to cancel, don't be upset or take it personally. Most importantly, don't stop reaching out.

Check In. Remember the person who is sick and the caregiver. A quick phone call, a text, a card or a message on social media can make all the difference. Every day can be overwhelming and without these quick check-ins, they can feel lonely and forgotten.

Stay Involved. Dealing with a chronic illness, is a daily, on-going struggle that can last for a lifetime. The patient and caregiver need help and encouragement forever.

This health journey is tough on everybody. We need to make sure we are working together as a team to make it through the storm.

"God doesn't miss anything. He knows perfectly well all the love you've shown him by helping the needy Christians, and that you keep at it."
Hebrews 6:10

Laura's Story

I'll never forget when Todd approached me to discuss his funeral arrangements. I was stunned at first, and didn't feel ready to talk about it, but I remembered the challenges we faced when my momma passed away and knew we needed to face this head on.

Todd and I have had long conversations about this. Honestly, while it was emotionally challenging to discuss this in the face of Todd's illness, knowing Todd's deepest wishes, should I be faced with his death, offers me a sense of comfort and relief.

Todd keeps an updated and saved document on his phone where I can easily find his latest wishes. I will not be faced with making difficult decisions in the midst of grief which will give me the strength and peace to follow through on his wishes.

I have been proactive in encouraging others to discuss end-of-life decisions while their loved ones are healthy. I am often faced with silence when I share that Todd and I have made funeral plans and fully paid for them.

Listen, as Christians, we all look forward to heaven, to walking through the pearly gates onto streets of gold, yet we seem to have selective amnesia about our mortality. To discuss death is not giving up faith in God or his ability to keep us healthy and alive. Death is a guaranteed event in this life. Not talking about it, doesn't change that.

I don't say this to minimize the pain we feel when we experience the loss of friends and loved ones. I know from personal experience that loss, and the possibility of loss, can be overwhelming. Talking about it and having a plan can make it easier on everyone involved.

In a hectic world, where life can bombard us, this is one less thing to pile up on my emotions. I can be more present, not distant or distracted, and experience the special moments that become warm, comforting, and soothing memories that last a lifetime.

While I am grateful for every moment I have with Todd, let me share with you an experience that is memorable for different reasons.

You may recall Todd sharing about a friend who after asking about Todd's health responded with, "Well, he lasted this long."

This was a colleague who knew Todd from his Juvenile Justice days, whom I hadn't seen in quite a while. I was taken aback by her less-than-warm response.

I want to share with you that I have chosen to allow the "crazy things people say" to soften me, rather than harden me.

I never know what someone else is going through. They may be having a rough day, and their insensitive comments may have nothing to do with me. Sometimes people struggle and suffer high levels of stress which diminishes their coping skills. Sometimes they just have a different frame of reference. Life is too short to bicker, and grace can go a long way in giving others a pass when they need it.

SHOEMAKER

Chapter Seven

The Willing Advocate

"Where's the Patient?"

I sincerely hope that the previous chapter equipped you with many practical ways to show your support to friends and family facing chronic illness. While it is important for a patient to know they are surrounded by others who care, one of the most important things a patient, and their primary caregiver, must know is how to advocate for themselves.

Let me tell you about a time I advocated for what was important to me. A health journey like mine, more often than not, includes lots and lots (did I say lots?), oh yeah, and lots of medications. As we all know, these medications come with lots and lots (okay, okay, I won't go there again) of side effects. For me, one of those side effects has been Type 2 diabetes.

Unfortunately, during one of my many hospital stays, I had a serious run-in with these side effects. I buzzed the nurses' station and reported through the crackly monitor, "I am feeling extremely dizzy and weak."

A few minutes later the nurse sailed into my room, took one look at me, and said, "Let's check a few things out."

One of those things was blood sugar level, which turned out to be extremely high, over 600.

The nurse quickly called my doctor who ordered me a medication to bring my blood sugar down, which worked too well, and my sugar plummeted below 50. My doctor arrived right about this time and ordered me to ICU.

"Please don't send me to ICU," I begged.

"I'm sorry, Todd, but ICU is the best place to monitor you," the doctor replied, and I knew he was right.

Next thing I know, the nurse pushes a wheelchair into my room. "No way!" I objected. "If I have to go to ICU, there is no way I am going in a wheelchair."

The doctor and nurse saw there was no arguing with me, so Laura and I collected my belongings and walked into the ICU. As we entered the unit, the nurses looked around in confusion and asked, "Where's the patient?"

I raised my hand. "Here I am."

I wish I had taken a picture of their faces. Priceless.

Five days later, I walked out of ICU. As I write this book, I am happy to report I no longer have Diabetes.

But I share this humorous little story to assure you that you have a voice, and that it is not just okay, but important that you use it. You may even be thinking that I should have just allowed the nurse to push me to ICU in a wheelchair, but my goal throughout my health journey has been to be as strong and healthy as I can in the moment. If I can make it on my own two feet, that is what I am going to do.

I am blessed in the fact that not only am I now a strong advocate for myself, but I am supported by my wonderful wife and caregiver. No patient or caregiver starts out being a health advocate! Unexpected and long-term health issues somewhat force you into this role. I thank God everyday Laura and I chose to embrace this new role.

When we began this crazy, beautiful journey back in 2002, we had no idea what we were doing. We walked out of doctors' appointments scratching our heads, trying to understand what on earth the doctors just said to us. It was not long before we were no longer willing to sit quietly for a mere five minutes of the doctor's time. We showed up at doctors' appointments equipped with pen, paper, and lots of questions fueled by our research.

Some doctors welcomed our approach with enthusiasm. Some doctors literally rolled their eyes when they saw us coming. Guess what we did with those doctors? We fired them! That's right, we fired them. Did you know you can fire your doctor? You can!

We always did it in a civil manner, but the bottom line is your doctor works for you. You are not a number, and every patient deserves the time they need to fully understand the health issues they are facing. If a doctor is not willing to listen and engage with you, find a doctor who will.

Over the years, we've learned a few things that work for us, and we'd like to share them with you in the hopes they will be helpful if you ever find yourself in the doctor's office.

- *Write down your questions before you arrive – doctors' appointments always move at a fast pace.*
- *Equip yourself to walk out of every appointment feeling empowered.*
- *Take someone with you – a second set of eyes and ears is always a good thing.*

When I first became sick in 2002, I would go to the doctor on my own. Laura called after appointments to ask what the doctor had to say. Most of the time, I either didn't remember, wasn't quite sure, or didn't know how to explain it. Not only that, but I forgot to ask the questions that were important to Laura.

I've learned to bring Laura or a friend to every medical appointment or procedure with me. We have a very special friend, Jean, who fills in when Laura can't be there. Jean is a valuable member of Team Todd. She's been to so many appointments with me, people think she's my sister until she speaks, and they hear her English accent. And she does speak! Laura trusts Jean to be there when she can't, to be thorough and ask all the questions Laura would ask if she were there.

After your appointment, have a discussion with the person who accompanied you – talk about what you both heard and understood during the appointment.

Laura and I go to dinner or lunch together and discuss what we heard and understood at the appointment. If Laura is not available, a close friend comes and does the same. Each perception adds to the full picture and reveals any areas where there might be questions.

Our friend Jean, even researches the options – medications, treatments, etc. She is always willing to have an honest conversation with us about side effects.

Remember, overwhelming information that is coupled with an emotional charge, can easily equal misunderstandings. These post-appointment meetings minimize difficulties and maximize future interactions with the medical team.

Keep an updated list of your medications, other doctors, past surgeries, tests/scans, and allergies. Who can remember all that stuff off the top of your head? Definitely not me!

Laura has created a handy information sheet that includes my name, date of birth, current medications, diagnoses, spouse information, warnings and specific directions, all of my current doctors, their specialties and contact information, any medical devices implanted with serial and model numbers, when the implant procedure occurred along with any cautions, medical allergies and reactions, any drugs that are contraindicated for my condition, and guidance for triage at my many Emergency Room visits.

Not only is there no possibility I can retain all this information, the doctors and nurses appreciate it, and it has been a lifesaver. On one ER visit, our friend Jean noticed the doctor was ordering a medication I was allergic to and spoke up. I wasn't in good shape and wouldn't have been able to do that for myself. Unless you have no choice, never go to the ER alone. Have a key team member who is balanced and emotionally strong who can be of support with you every time.

Never be afraid to ask for a second opinion. This is your life!

This is a lesson we learned with the very first specialist we saw. When I was diagnosed with arthritis, the doctor prescribed a lot of experimental drugs.

I had an appointment with him the week we found out I had a tumor. When we arrived at the appointment, we let the nurse know, and the doctor refused to see us. I can't help but wonder if he believed the experimental drugs were responsible.

Do your research. If your doctor is on the board for pharmaceutical companies, it may be a conflict of interest.

Surround yourself with a good team – this includes family, friends, and medical team.

Every long-term patient needs a strong support team. Our friend, Jean, is a great example of a team member you can trust, who is willing to make sacrifices. She drives us to appointments, take trips with us, she has even missed her daughter's birthday to be there for us. Jean and her husband, Chris, live close to the hospital and host Laura when I've been admitted. They treat her like an honored guest, have hot meals waiting for her, and keep her comfortable in every way. They have also bestowed upon us the honor of being godparents to their children.

Jean doesn't have any special credentials or training; she has MS. Which brings me to an important point, another person who is ill can still be a great support. When building your team, don't knock me off the list. But remember, not every team member can be like Jean. It is important to allow unsupportive team members to fade away.

Let your medical team know what does and doesn't work for you when you must have a test, procedure, or surgery. Most of the time they will be happy to assist and accommodate. If not, remember you can fire them.

Never be afraid to speak up and let your medical team know what works for you. When I had a sore throat three weeks after surgery, I learned that I need smaller tubing. Now, I let my medical team know.

When I was in the hospital once my IV needed to be replaced, which as you might guess can be a nightmare. Two and a half hours and eight sticks later, covered in bandages and bruises, I told my oncologist they couldn't find a vein.

"Why didn't they use your port?" he asked incredulously.

"I don't have one," I replied.

"You will this afternoon," he stated emphatically.

And I did! If you need an IV frequently, a port is extremely helpful. I wish I had it sooner. Again, do your research and ASK for what you need.

Another incredible way that you can become a health advocate is by *helping others along the way*. Laura and I decided early on in my health journey that we wanted to help and encourage others going through their own journeys. There have been times we have been lost and overwhelmed in our own journey, but we have never regretted our choice to help others.

I have had the honor of praying with fellow patients on their worst days, and the honor of rejoicing with them when they have experienced a victory. Laura has had the opportunity to walk beside so many other caregivers.

I often say, "Caregivers have the toughest job." As a patient, I know my job. It's simply to get better. A caregiver has many roles. Laura has become my health advocate, my chauffer, my cheerleader, my voice, and so much more. She still works a demanding full-time job, and even went back to school and earned her Masters' Degree during this.

Yet, we recognize our ability to help others is evidence of the many wonderful people who have supported us.

Will every patient and caregiver become as involved as Laura and I have over the years? Maybe, maybe not. But we are here to encourage you to use the lessons you learn throughout the course of your health journey to benefit someone else going through their journey or struggle in life. No one should ever have to walk alone!

"Nothing, you see, is impossible with God."

Luke 1:37

Laura's Story

When we experience a life challenge for the first time, we don't often know how to respond. Challenges often bring about an emotional response which makes it difficult to tap into our problem-solving skills. I encourage you to identify your resources and your support. It's different for everyone. Talk with others who've faced these challenges; gain insight from their experiences. Take what is helpful and leave the rest.

I have found it incredibly helpful when facing our medical challenges to write everything down. My mind was so full balancing life – work details, doctors' comments, appointment dates for exams, procedures, therapies, and the list goes on. I needed to have a process to document it all.

Record key details so you can reference back to them when needed. Find a system for recording information in a way that works for you.

Do you notice a theme? *Whatever you do, find what works for you, but you don't need to do it alone!*

Todd and I made it a habit to have a meal after appointments and procedures to discuss what we heard. Sometimes we invited a dear friend to come with us to help retain information and ask the questions we didn't know to ask... or think to ask.

When the medical professional you work with is unable or unwilling to answer your questions, consider finding a new provider.

If your dentist didn't clean your teeth well, or worse, didn't use enough anesthesia, you would fire your dentist. If your accountant neglected to file your taxes, you wouldn't stick with them. Would you continue to go to a mechanic who took your money yet failed to repair your car? I hope not!

If the professional is not supporting you in the way you need, move on, find relief. Feel free to fire them and find a new one – one that will answer your questions and meet your needs!

Over time, we moved from being timid to confident, when it came to excellent medical care. Todd's life depended on it!

We trusted the Lord for strength, and we asked for wisdom. We believed God was in control and He was faithful to guide us to the right resources for support and care.

When we made changes, and we did, it was done in a way that treated others with dignity and respect. Todd's mission field is in hospitals and doctor's offices. It was important to us to respect the doctors, nurses, the receptionist at the front desk, and other patients in the waiting room. Our respect reflects our faith in a loving, caring God.

He has promised us that ALL things work together for good for those that love God and are called according to His purpose, and that's us.

This journey has brought about plenty of challenges, but we have learned valuable lessons from our struggles. It is our hope to support and encourage others as we share what has been given to us.

Chapter Eight

Becoming a Caregiver

"Honey, whatever you want to do!"

Laura's Story

Being a caregiver for Todd has brought me to a new journey in life. My role is so much more than just a wife now. This is what God has called me to do, and I work to honor that commitment.

People often comment that I am so patient, kind, and respectful. It is sweet of them to say. What they don't realize is this... I make the decision to be respectful and kind toward Todd, being patient of his limitations, and accommodating him without enabling. Cherishing our marriage, our friendship and our commitment to each other is a deliberate choice.

Every day, I make a conscience choice to keep an attitude of honoring Todd in the tough times, honoring his ability to make his own decisions. This means I am deliberate in preserving his dignity to make decisions on his own, to help when he asked for help, and staying committed to the journey God has for us.

Over the years I have found peace in knowing that God has called me to be Todd's helpmate. There ARE times when I have the negative self-talk and get overwhelmed. Through counseling and self-care, I've been able to build my coping skills. Sure, occasionally I still fight against negative thoughts or attitudes, but I make an intentional effort to find and hold onto gratefulness.

There is always something to be grateful for even in the midst of storms, struggles, or my heartache. I look for those moments, and when I find them, they help my heart and restore my mind.

Gratitude brings me life and rejuvenation when I am faced with desperation or loneliness. This can only come from trusting the Lord, being grateful, and finding peaceful moments by focusing on the good things that we have been blessed with.

I continue to remind myself that all things work together for good to those that love God. He promises that I can do all things through Christ who strengthens me.

Remembering and reciting my life scriptures keeps me grounded in the truth. Proverbs 3:5-6 says, "Trust in the Lord with all your heart, don't lean on your own understanding. In all your ways, acknowledge Him and He will direct your path." What a great promise.

When it comes to caregiving it's a matter of *acts from the heart*. I am constantly checking my motives and intentions to identify when bitterness or resentment surfaces. It is human nature for bitterness and resentment to surface, so you must be vigilant to watch for any signs and check your reactions.

Several times in our marriage, there have been declines in Todd's health. With each new level of decline, there's a grieving process of what our life was up to that point. I have learned to face and accept the new normal, and properly deal with grief as it comes up. It is only though Christ's love, strength, and encouragement that I am steadfast, relying on God's strength to carry me through.

Change is not always easy for me to embrace. Once I have adjusted to a new normal and begin enjoying my new comfort zone, a decline in Todd's health can leave me with a sense of disappointment at the loss.

Hope in God is my bridge from despair to life and thriving. It's like the difference between having oxygen or suffocating. Holding on to hope and gratitude is my daily goal. When that goal gets fuzzy or extinguished, I then struggle with despair.

I am frequently too hard on myself, thinking I am not doing enough, not doing it soon enough, or kicking myself for not thinking of a solution sooner. All of this is critical self-talk. I continuously work on being kind to myself, or as the professionals put it, self-compassion. It is easier to offer grace and mercy to others than to yourself.

My ongoing struggles with depression are compounded by a strong feeling that I am responsible for the wellbeing of others. I love and support Todd, but I am constantly analyzing my assistance. Does he need me to do this or that for him? Am I giving unsolicited help to satisfy my own need to care for him? I want to preserve his dignity and allow him to make his own decisions about his needs. I must remind myself to wait for him to ask for my help.

As a teenager my dad would encourage me to take care of myself. He saw compassionate qualities in me, which at times would risk my own wellbeing. He would tell me, "Now, Sweetheart, I know you want to help your friends who are hurting. You see a friend stuck in a deep hole, you can't help them by jumping in there with them. You need to find ways to help, from above the hole, assisting them out of the hole." Of course, he was right.

Depression is an illness, not a weakness. With illness, one can seek help. This is part of my self-care, I see a counselor and get medical care, as needed.

Over the years it has been important for me to remember both soul-care and self-care, learning that it is truly loving and giving towards Todd when I replenish my body and soul. Much to my surprise, art has become therapy for me and is a regular part of my life.

Todd is so caring and gracious, he makes sure I have time for my art and time with friends. It might be a girls' night or weekend away. He has even sent me off on cruises with family for rest and relaxing. We take care of each other.

I've had to learn and practice self-care. Self-care models I found online gave me visuals, prompting my creativity, and some ideas of healthy ways to care for myself. I try to focus on ALL the components of self-care in my life, physical, psychological, professional, emotional, spiritual and personal. It helps me to continue to give while being a wife, being a full-time employee, being the breadwinner, preserving the marriage, and being a friend.

If you have ever flown, you've sat through the preflight safety instructions given by the airline attendants. Should oxygen become necessary, they assure you the mask will drop down to provide it, BUT they admonish you to put your own mask on first, before attempting to assist those around you. Why? Well, you can't very well help those beside you if you have passed out from a lack of oxygen.

The same is true in caregiving. Burnout is a legitimate and challenging risk. Healthy coping skills are critical for wellness. As a caregiver, I can't emphasis enough the importance of self-care. Nurturing myself, with healthy balance, is a loving act to my family.

Todd's Story

I have walked the halls of a hospital many times during my health journey, stopping and praying with many of my fellow patients. It is part of my journey and God has called me to bring comfort to them. The hardest moments are when I visit someone walking their journey alone. It makes me appreciate the beautiful gift God gave me. My wife Laura.

It is hard to put into words everything Laura means to me. She has taken on many roles during this journey. Laura has been my friend, cheerleader, advocate, chauffeur and all-around caregiver, for most of our marriage. The amazing thing is, she has done it without complaining. She truly took the wedding vows *through sickness and health* seriously. I could not and would not want to walk this journey without her. My prayer is that everyone walking through a storm would have a Laura walking beside them.

"I know what I'm doing. I have it all planned out – plans to take care of you, not abandon you, plans to give you the future you hope for."
Jeremiah 29:11

SHOEMAKER

Needs to be reworked

Chapter Nine

Becoming Blessed Overcomers

"We have learned so much along the way!"

This crazy, beautiful journey has been filled with so many lessons and gifts. Every struggle has had a silver lining, so each day we decide to see the positives. We want to share some of these with you, to encourage you in whatever journey you are on.

If I could only share one thing with you it would be this... never allow your circumstances to define you. I have learned that I am not just a person dealing with multiple health issues. I am not just the crazy guy who ran a thousand miles in a year. NOT just the man who refuses to die... NO, I am a husband, a friend, and an overcomer. More importantly, I am a child of the most-high God. THAT is what defines me.

Something that continually amazes us is our ability to overcome anything. After all, I became a marathoner after NOT running for twenty years AND ran a thousand miles in a year with Parkinson's and undiagnosed Myasthenia Gravis! That is the God I serve. I encourage you to never allow an obstacle to keep you from being all God wants you to be.

Early on we decided to focus on the positives of this journey. We could have spent our time on the negatives asking WHY. Why did I get sick? Why is my life so full of doctor appointments and hospital stays? I could dwell on those questions all day, but it would not change my current health issues. In fact, it would probably make them worse.

By deciding to focus on the positives, I became an Abolitionist, a Missionary, a Speaker, and an Encourager. As a result of our decision to focus on others, Laura and I became Patient Advocates. WOW, when you look at all the positives of this journey, no wonder we don't have time to spend on the negatives. It has been a choice; you can make the same choice for yourself.

I have said it already, but it is worth repeating, I am truly blessed to be married to Laura West Shoemaker. We never had big disagreements before I got sick, perhaps we were still newlyweds or perhaps we were just blessed. During our journey we have seen other patients and their families struggle as the stress of an illness caused them to argue over the littlest things. Laura and I heard stories of a healthy spouse leaving because they could no longer take the enormity of the situation.

Determined to not let that happen to us, we made the decision to not turn small things into big things and vowed to never allow the big things to tear us apart. We don't bicker over the little things, we focus on the big picture. We made a commitment to each other when we got married and we are not going to let health issues interfere with our beautiful journey. That is not always easy when a loved one is dealing with major health issues, but we are proof that by the grace of God, it is possible.

It would not be possible without those who journey with us. As you recall, I had to retire early due to my health issues. For a majority of that first year, Laura and I survived on her paycheck while I waited to see if I qualified for Social Security Disability. During that long year, so many of our friends and even strangers blessed us financially. We would receive cards with well wishes and money. Money that we never asked for, but God knew we needed. It was one of the toughest years we have faced, it is also one of the most rewarding as we watched God provide in unimaginable ways. He is so faithful.

Not only did we feel loved and cared for by the financial support that year, we also learned how important others would be to our survival. For countless hours family and friends have sat with me during treatments or hospital stays, because Laura had to be at work. More times than we can count, people have brought food to our house, so an exhausted Laura would not have to cook. Eventually we lost count of how many times family and friends sent messages of prayer and support. God never intended for us to walk this crazy, beautiful journey alone.

Surrounded by family and friends who want to feed us, the variety of tasty meals has been wonderful, but the Christian Help Guide must say "Bring Brownies" because the variety of desserts... not so much. Laura and I received so many brownies that we had to give some away. Don't get me wrong, we love brownies but after a while it was too much. In appreciation and love, my tip to those providing meals, add some variety to your dessert game.

During this crazy, beautiful journey, we have learned the importance of truly living every minute. We eat dessert (except brownies), surround ourselves with family and friends, and turn medical trips into adventure trips.

When faced with a life-threatening diagnosis, some people crawl into a corner and stop living. From the beginning, Laura and I have embraced new experiences. There have been many trips across the country to different hospitals, so we made them into adventures. Local people think we are on vacation because we are having so much fun!

Some think we are crazy for all the trips we take. Is traveling hard on my body? YES. It usually takes me weeks to recover from these trips, but I wouldn't trade those trips for anything. Laura and I have made so many amazing memory moments during this crazy, beautiful journey. Just because you are dealing with a storm in life, it doesn't mean you have to stop enjoying life and living.

This whole journey, and this book, is based on hope. I would not be writing these words if not for His hope. We all face some tough times in life. That is a given, but I want to encourage you to hold onto the promises of God and His hope during those times. He will never leave you during your worst storms.

"That's why we can be so sure that every detail in our lives of love
for God is worked into something good."
Romans 8:28

Laura's Story

It has never been easy to let others help me; I have had to learn the art of accepting help from others. It means accepting my own weaknesses, realizing I can't do it all myself, and I shouldn't try to. Over time I have developed tools to help me practice acceptance, perhaps they will help you as well.

Identify the kind of support you need. If you have thought out what you truly need, it is easier to verbalize it when someone asks what they can do to help. When someone offers help in an area you never considered, but could use, accept the offer.

If you find yourself refusing help, try to identify if pride or embarrassment is behind the refusal. Pray that God will help you to accept support from others.

The bottom line... when it comes to support for you and your family during times of need, become comfortable saying, "Yes, please."

During stressful times, it is almost guaranteed that people will say the wrong things. As humans we want to comfort and offer verbal support, but we often miss the mark. We have learned to fight against being offended when the wrong words are used. When you are struggling in the storms of life, try to practice selective amnesia when this happens. Stress and fatigue will lower tolerance and challenge your coping skills. You will hear some unhelpful things and it is easy to get offended. Practice a kind response that you can use; it will help preserve valuable relationships.

I continually hold onto scriptures like The Lord's Prayer... "forgive us our sins, as we forgive those who sin against us." Grace and mercy are free gifts, to all of us from God. Give the same gift to others with a kind response.

I have learned that I don't have to be right all the time and I don't have the answers all the time either. Often, I convince myself that I am right, when in fact, I misunderstood a situation and really don't have the answers. At times, I am truly right, but what does it hurt to leave the conversation alone and allow another person to believe what they believe. I work at being a peacemaker, *"blessed are the peacemakers."*

This crazy, beautiful journey has taught me many lessons. In fact, I continue to learn and grow. It is my prayer that this book will give you guidance that you may benefit from the things I have learned, but most of all, I pray it gives you hope.

Chapter Ten

The Power of Love

"We'd rather have medical issues than marital issues!"

You've been reading about our medical journey, but it's not the whole story, we want you to know about the amazing love story we are living!

Laura and I met at church. Every Sunday morning, I would hold my godson, David, but before I had a chance to meet Laura, she fell in love with that cute little bundle. Thanks for helping me out, David!

It was not until my first singles event that Laura and I met. The event was a bike ride, or rollerblading if you were brave enough, on the Palm Beach Trail. After cruising the bike trail for a while, the group decided to have some lunch. Laura struck up a conversation, and we chatted for a few hours. To be honest, neither of us left that conversation thinking we had met the person we would spend the rest of our lives with... that would have been a great story right!?! We did leave thinking we had started a nice friendship with another single person.

Obviously, I married that friend. Somehow, I knew it was important to let Laura have the wedding of her dreams, so we started planning a wedding, even before we set a date. All I can say is WOW, I had no idea how stressful it would be, and it kept growing into a larger and larger event. Finally, we both decided that eloping was looking very attractive to us, and we ditched the wedding plans for a different adventure.

There was already a betting pool at Laura's work about the date, so we didn't tell anyone. You guessed it, we eloped. Her coworkers knew something was up that day because Laura could hardly contain herself. We managed to keep the secret and really enjoyed sneaking away to get married.

The very next morning Laura sat straight up and proclaimed, "I got married without telling my mother!"

She looked startled and a bit upset, so I did the only rational thing I could think of. We packed the car and headed to her mother's house. We spent a lovely weekend, on our honeymoon, at her parents' house. We still enjoy telling that story!

That first singles event was in January of 1999 and by September, we were saying our wedding vows. Yes, it was quick, but it was the best decision of my life. Okay, second best decision behind giving my life to God! Aside from my health journey, we have had some amazing experiences and created many beautiful memories. We share an amazing love for each other, what a precious gift it is.

In 2003, after settling into married life, we decided to adopt a puppy. LuLu was a cute little basset hound, a real pill to be sure, but we loved her. She cried every day when we left her and went to work. Someone suggested we adopt another puppy so she would have a friend during the day. For some reason we thought this was a great idea... and Savannah came to live with us. Basset hound puppy number two.

We loved those puppies, but let's just say, there is a reason Laura and I never had children. We were terrible puppy parents. We let those two babies rule our lives.

Not knowing what my treatments could entail, upon learning about the babies, my doctors had suggested that two puppies might not be the best idea. I felt confident our babies would be fine and that the doctors were just being overly cautious.

Being the worried wife, Laura had warned that I should not walk more than one dog at time. One day after my biopsy, I took both dogs for a walk, yes, together. Spotting some girls playing ball, both dogs took off running and I hit the ground. Thankfully the girls caught the runaway hounds for me, but I was sore and had to admit to Laura that she had been right. It broke our hearts, but we started to consider the doctor's advice.

You remember, of course, that our moms came to take care of us when I first got sick. Well that included our two babies, LuLu and Savannah. Laura's mother loved both the puppies, but she really loved Savannah. Of course, Savannah was well behaved while our LuLu was... not so much. Laura and I take full responsibility for that.

Laura's mother was considering taking our Savannah home to live with her, so she prayed about it. While she was praying, "God, give me a sign if I should take this dog home with me," Savannah jumped up on the couch and pooped on one of the pillows right in front of her. I am not lying. Savannah, our angel, had never done anything like that before. Momma West took it as a sign and decided to NOT take home the adorable puppy.

Thankfully, some friends of ours knew a lady with 15 acres and a basset hound rescue. So, after many tears, our wild little puppies moved up in the world. Honestly, they love running and playing at their new home in the country.

Prior to meeting the love of my life, I had been volunteering at an inner-city ministry called Urban Youth Impact. I truly loved working with these young people. That is where I met Ricky Aiken. At the time I had no clue how this young man would change my life.

After Laura and I were married, I sort of lost touch with Ricky, only seeing each other on occasion. On Ricky's 18th birthday I mentioned to Laura that Urban Youth Impact had given Ricky his first birthday cake ever! She could not believe it, Laura loves birthdays! She was determined that this young man, whom she had never met, was going to have the best birthday ever. Don't you love her heart?

We made the arrangements to pick up Ricky and celebrate his birthday with him. Laura went all out with a luncheon and a cake, then we took him shopping. We were struck by how humble Ricky was about the whole birthday celebration. It touched our hearts and that was the day we decided to unofficially adopt him.

Ricky is now in his early 30's and making a tremendous difference in his neighborhood. Several years ago, he started an organization called Inner City Innovators, to help end gun violence in his community. Laura and I are so proud of this young man we call our son.

Laura and I have been blessed to have so many wonderful people walk this journey with us; we could not do this without our team. It started when I was running marathons. Team Todd would be at the side lines or the finish line to cheer me on and celebrate with us. In time, we came to realize that every one of the team members had overcome something. It seemed natural to change the name to Team Blessed Overcomer. It would take several chapters to name all the individuals who have been a part of the team during our crazy, beautiful journey, but they know who they are. Laura and I are honored they decided to walk this journey with us. It has not been an easy one but is has been filled with incredible memories.

"You're my cave to hide in, my cliff to climb. Be my safe leader, be my true mountain guide."
Psalm 31:3

Laura's Story

I am convinced that my wonderful marriage can be attributed to my sweet momma's prayers. When I was a young adult my mom would pray for my future husband. Together we prayed and trusted that God would bring him into my life, even though I would date all the wrong guys while I waited. We prayed that God would bless him and prepare him to be a Godly, loving husband. I cherish the gift of a praying mother, trusting God's best for all three of her children.

When Todd and I first met, my office family worked hard to coach me on all things sport related. I didn't grow up around sports or acquire a love for them, but Todd was a huge sports fan! They taught me just enough to allow me to follow a conversation with

Todd.

One day my boss gave me tickets to a hockey game. She was a season ticket holder but couldn't go that night for some reason. I was so excited but had no way of contacting Todd during the work day. This was before I had his cell number and I had to find my new friend and invite him!

I recalled a conversation about his work and knew he was a manager in the Civil Courts Office of the main court house. I knew WHERE to find him, but I also remembered he was not allowed to take personal calls at work.

So, I called the office and impersonated someone. I said my neighbor had taken my cat and wouldn't give it back to me. YES, I lied, desperately needing to tell Todd about the hockey tickets. I said a man named Shoemaker was helping with my case, and could I please speak to him. It worked!

Todd was shocked, but I quickly distracted him with the offer of hockey tickets for that night. He was excited and agreed to join me for the evening. It was during that exciting game, with the crashing of masks and the slapping of hockey sticks, that cupid struck me. Until that night I had convinced myself that Todd was a good friend, but I was not interested in dating him. During that game, God changed my heart and I was overwhelmingly attracted to him. What a great night! I had no idea who won the game, all I knew was Todd had won my heart.

One of our first official dates was a baseball game. Of course, I had no clue what was happening on the field. We sat so close to each other, our elbows were touching, and butterflies were fluttering in my heart. I could feel the electricity between us.

During the game Todd went to get us some snacks. After he left a little lady leaned over to me and said, "How long have you been married?" I was shocked and responded that it was a new relationship.

Apparently, when I had gone to the bathroom, the lady had asked Todd the same question. He thought it was all a set-up and I was the mastermind behind it. After all, I managed to find him at the court house by impersonating a cat owner, just to ask him out!

It happened more than once while we were dating; people thought we were married. One evening we were out to dinner, just holding hands and talking, enjoying each other's company. A stranger came to our table, "Excuse me for interrupting, but how long have you been married? I see a glow around you."

We were both freaked out, I don't recall how we answered. At the time we didn't realize we had met our soul mates, but everyone else seemed to know. After years of prayer for direction, it was a relief when God brought us from just dating to knowing we were meant for each other.

When we dated, became engaged and married within a short 9 months, God gave me peace about starting my life with Todd, so we simply eloped. It was the best decision of my life. Such joy, peace and a quick beginning to our life together.

Chapter Eleven

The Power of Living

"The man who refuses to die."

Laura and I reminisce often about our crazy, beautiful journey and enjoy entertaining each other by recounting the funny stuff. One of the things we still laugh about is those crazy things people say, like the names they have given me. Over the years I've had some pretty cool nicknames!

One of the first names given to me was *Genetic Freak*. One of my doctors gave me that name. Apparently, many of the things going on in my body were not normal... I was indeed a genetic freak. I always liked that name, it sounded like an awesome band. Laura even had some Genetic Freak signs made for one of my marathons. You can probably imagine the strange looks and questions we got. It gave us the opportunity to share why I got the name and how God was blessing me!

One night we were sitting in church and my pastor, Coach Tom Mullins, introduced me to someone as *The Man Who Refuses to Die*. We didn't give it a second thought until people started coming up and saying, "Aren't you the guy who refuses to die?" Some people don't care for the name, but I love it. Coach Mullins gave me that nickname because he knew God was not finished with me yet.

Probably my favorite nickname of all is *The Blessed Overcomer*. It wasn't from a particular person, but we have seen God's blessings over and over during this crazy, beautiful journey and several people have called me an overcomer. We have experienced so many amazing blessings and overcome many obstacles along the way... the name is fitting. When it became possible to write our story and publish our book, we knew what the name had to be.

When I got sick again in 2009, I had two prayers. I prayed that I would never LOOK sick and I prayed that I would never ACT sick. Lying in ICU, I don't know why but those were my prayers, and God has used those prayers to help me share His love.

Remember those crazy things that people say? I can't tell you how many times people have said I don't look or act sick. Those two answered prayers have allowed me to share my testimony with people who would never open a Bible or walk into a place of worship. I had no idea how two simple prayers would change the lives of so many.

This journey has been a crazy roller coaster ride. When Laura and I walked into the doctor's office in 2002, we never imagined how long the journey would be. I believe both of us are better people because of our journey. It comes down to the choice we made; we made the conscious decision to thrive and flourish, whatever that looked like for us.

We could have chosen to stay quiet and not encourage others, no one would have blamed us. Think of everything we would have missed!

What does our future hold? We don't know, but God does. I believe he still has great plans for us. We will continue to listen AND obey. We will continue to stand by the decision to thrive and flourish.

"Live carefree before God; he is most careful with you."
1 Peter 5:7

Laura's Story

I was 30 years old when Todd and I were married, I was so excited to say goodbye to the single life. For me, dating was a search for my soulmate. The title of Wife was an honor I had prayed and longed for. While we were dating, friends and family knew that Todd was the one for me. Even my parents gave their blessing, which spoke volumes. What an exciting and wonderful time.

In a lifetime of expectations about marriage, it never occurred to me that I would take on the role and title of caregiver. Todd is so easy to love, even in his struggles he continues to be considerate, respectful, fun-loving, and humorous. In fact, humor has been one of his strengths. He makes me laugh, day after day, it keeps us smiling.

I recall one trip to the doctor that we still laugh about today. Todd had a tube that needed to be removed and this simple procedure could be done at the office. While I preferred to wait outside the room, the doctor insisted that I join them, and trying to be the supportive wife, I agreed to be in the room.

As the doctor chatted with us, he began to remove the metal staples that held the tube in place. I'm not clear why but staples seemed to be flying everywhere. I still remember the ping of the metal staples hitting things.

Then, when the doctor tried to remove the tube, it wouldn't come out! Scrunching his face and gritting his teeth, he tried to pull it out, but it would not budge. Finally, the doctor put his foot on the exam table for leverage, but to no avail. The tube would not be moved; it had to be removed surgically. Poor Todd, I'm sure it was painful, but we laugh and laugh about that doctor's visit.

I've always enjoyed the names given to Todd, they remind me to enjoy the humor in life. The Man Who Refuses to Die is one of my favorite titles. Of course, I realize that Todd is NOT immortal, but during the times that Todd has faced death, I held onto hope that God would give me a little more time with him here on earth. I understand death and that young people sometimes die. Struggling with the possibility more times than I care to count, I held onto Todd's title, praying he would refuse to die yet again.

Genetic Freak is my other favorite title for Todd, always such a great conversation starter! When people hear about Todd's struggles and that he also ran 1,000 miles in one year... God gets the glory. It is a testament to God's goodness, grace, and strength.

This journey has built my faith in the Lord, teaching me to trust God in all things, regardless of the facts: a failing body, near the brink of death, but God is bigger than what we see before our eyes.

I love my Genetic Freak, The Man Who Refuses to Die (defying science at times), and to God be the glory, the Blessed Overcomer.

SHOEMAKER

Chapter Twelve

The Power of Choice & Perspective

"It's not my turn to eat."

I truly believe my purpose in this life is to love and encourage others. It's what my health journey is all about, using my experiences to help encourage others going through their own storms.

Over the past 17 years my faith has grown so much. I'm not sure I would be the man I am today if not for this journey. It sounds crazy, but I would not change a thing. I have had to learn to trust God during so many storms. Trust HIM when the diagnosis was not something I wanted to hear. The amazing gift that came from it all is a deep sense of compassion for others.

Prior to getting sick in 2002, I remember taking a spiritual gifting assessment. It's a bit embarrassing, but compassion was one of my lowest scores. I took the same test a few years ago and wouldn't you know it, one of my highest scores was in the area of compassion. Isn't that interesting?

In 2014, I started losing my appetite. At first that wasn't a bad thing, who couldn't stand to lose a few pounds, right? When I did eat, I would feel full after a few small bites of food. We didn't pay much attention to the issue until 2015, when I stopped getting hungry or thirsty at all. A series of tests diagnosed my condition, Gastroparesis. Not to bore you with medical jargon, it basically means my stomach muscles are paralyzed.

Eating and drinking became a problem; it was painful and NOT fun. An interesting experience in a culture so driven by food and drink. After several different medications had failed, the doctors decided it was time for a gastro pacemaker. Yes, it is just what it sounds like, a pacemaker for my stomach. The main purpose was to relieve some of the constant nausea associated with Gastroparesis. I am happy to report the pacemaker did its job! Since I still couldn't eat or drink, in 2017 the doctors inserted a feeding tube to nourish my body. My weight had gotten dangerously low and they only gave me a few weeks to live. I told you I have earned the nickname *The Blessed Overcomer*!

One of our favorite stories to tell is one about a feeding tube. They replace the tubes often, it's a short surgical procedure that I have become accustomed to. Early in that adventure, Laura was at work, so I was home alone that day. I was having a shower and I looked down just as my feeding tube fell OUT. Stunned, I grabbed the tube, washed it, sterilized it, and put it back in! Not sure how to react, I called Laura to explain the situation. After reassuring her I was fine she suggested I call the doctor for our next course of action. I called the office and the doctor said, "Eh, you're fine." We still chuckle about that one.

Our lives have been filled with humor, intrigue, and adventures. It has not always been easy to embrace God's timing or plan for us.

We all think our plan is best, admit it. I sometimes wonder if it makes God laugh. I thought God's plan was for me to run marathons to raise awareness about human trafficking. In fact, I had it all planned out, but God had a different plan. It is not the plan I would have chosen but going from long-distance runner to medical marvel has been quite an adventure.

Before I got sick, Laura and I had been pretty comfortable with our life. Maybe too comfortable, and my health issues forced us out of that comfort zone, into a whole new world. God chose us to encourage those who feel lost and confused by the storms of life. It was not our plan, but it is the plan that has changed my life. I encourage you to slow down and patiently wait on God's timing and plan for your life.

There's nothing like a 17-year health journey to teach you a few lessons. God has allowed me to endure and persevere more than I could have imagined possible. I truly believe God had me start running marathons back in 2004 to prepare me for this journey. During a marathon, runners suffer, no getting around it. The same is true in life. We all have periods of suffering.

My prayer for you is this, whatever you are facing at this moment, that you will seek God's guidance and direction. It is easier said than done. Please don't walk away from this book thinking my journey has been easy or that I have it all together. I do NOT. I am still a work in progress, but this journey HAS given me a different perspective on life. I no longer worry about the outward appearance; today I am more concerned about what's inside.

This journey made us look outside of ourselves and changed our attitudes about life. We stopped worrying about what others might think. We started to cherish time with friends and each other. We speak up more for the less fortunate. We jump in the car and take trips instead of just talking about it. We NEVER take a moment for granted. WOW, what a blessing!

I am still here today writing this book because of the prayers of many. Literally at death's door so many times, but the prayers of God's people have always brought me back. *The Man Who Refuses to Die* was surrounded by great prayer warriors who interceded on my behalf. Some people have been praying for me daily since 2002, never missing a day! I am humbled. My own prayer life has been strengthened by these prayer warriors. NEVER doubt how your prayers can change a life. Be bold in your prayers. Over the years, and even now as I continue to walk the halls of the hospital, no one has ever said NO to my offer of prayer for them.

As we finish this book, my health has taken another turn. I am facing some new challenges. My doctors are trying some short-term solutions, but only time will tell what God has planned. We believe that my healing will happen in heaven. It could be soon, or God might leave me here for several more years. Laura and I are at peace with whatever's next, God has the final say in our journey.

My prayer is that God will use our story, this book, to bless and encourage YOU! KNOW that He can sustain you in your storm, whatever you are facing. Trust Him, reach out to Him, and let the God who created you, be your peace.

"That's right. Because I, your God, have a firm grip on you and I'm not letting go. I'm telling you, don't panic. I'm right here to help you."
Isaiah 41:13

Laura's Story

When Todd was first struggling with eating, I became obsessed with finding answers and providing food that would pique his interest. After all, that was my job as his wife, to feed my husband. I had no idea it had nothing to do with his interest level in the actual food. He simply was not hungry. It was as if the mechanism in his brain, somewhere along the line, had switched "off" for hunger. Wouldn't that be a handy switch to have access to!

When medical doctors gave the condition a name, Gastroparesis, I was relieved from the stress and concern over it. We knew what the problem was so we could just fix it. Little did I realize, there was no easy or quick solution ahead. I didn't know this phase of our lives would become yet another *new normal.* Part of my medical knowledge resume, I have learned WAY too much about feeding tubes.

Todd and I have learned to embrace God's timing and plan in our lives. We are more open to the beautiful interruptions. When we don't know what is ahead, we take a deep breath knowing that God has gone before us, preparing the way. We are never alone. With all the titles and parts I play in this journey, my favorite is that of Todd's wife.

If you are struggling in life, my prayer is you find hope in the Lord Jesus Christ. He will provide strength, comfort, and peace, when life is overwhelming, just as He has done for us countless times. Claim your place as a Blessed Overcomer!

Letter from the Author

When this all started, we had no idea what an amazing journey this would be. God has been so faithful. He has used my ashes for His beauty, my brokenness for His glory. Lives have been touched and changed by hearing about His goodness!

We want to continue to be used by God to make a difference. Please feel free to reach out to us for encouragement and share your story. You can contact OC (Overcomer) anytime at (561) 632-3394 or TheBlessedOvercomer@gmail.com. You can also follow OC on his blog at www.TheBlessedOvercomer.org.

This is our story. We pray it encourages you. We pray it brings you hope in the midst of your own crazy, beautiful journey. Thank you for being a part of our story!

SHOEMAKER

38297221R00066

Made in the USA
Middletown, DE
08 March 2019